HOUSE OF COMMONS LIBRARY

LOCATIO

AUTHOR

Acc DATE

D0831248

HOUSE OF COMMONS LIBRARY

TO BE
DISPOSED
BY
AUTHORITY

House of Commons Library

54056001013090

The Story of Writing

Donald Jackson

The Story of Writing

Studio Vista
The Parker Pen Company

A Studio Vista book
published by Cassell Ltd,
35 Red Lion Square, London WC1R 4SG
and at Sydney, Auckland, Toronto, Johannesburg
an affiliate of
Macmillan Publishing Co., Inc., New York

Copyright © Donald Jackson 1981

First published in 1981

ISBN 0 289 70985 7

Edited and designed by Shuckburgh Reynolds Ltd,
8 Northumberland Place, London W2 5BS
on behalf of Parker Pen International,
15 Grosvenor Gardens, London SW1W 0BL

All rights reserved. No part of this publication
may be reproduced, stored in a retrieval system,
or transmitted in any form or by any means,
electronic, magnetic, mechanical, photographic or
otherwise, without prior permission in writing
from the publisher

Typesetting by SX Composing Ltd, Rayleigh, Essex
Printed and bound in Hong Kong by
Dai Nippon Printing Co. (H.K.) Ltd

Design: Nicholas Thirkell with Ashted Dastor
Picture research: Michael Gullick
Illustrations: Lawrence Mynott and Donald Jackson

Contents

List of Illustrations

Acknowledgements

This book grew out of a series of four films, "Alphabet: the Story of Writing", commissioned by Parker Pen International and produced and directed by Jeremy Bennett. Eighteen months of planning, script-writing and filming during 1978–80 meant that even before I started to write I had already received a lot of help and encouragement from others. I am grateful to Professor Julian Brown for suggestions on parts of the text, and to Philip Poole (His Nibs) for freely lending objects from his collection. The sources of other illustrations are acknowledged on pages 6–8. My especial thanks are due to Michael Gullick, who apart from gathering the illustrations has unselfishly shared both his time and his personal research material.

In a book which spans over 5,000 years of history I have had to rely on many sources other than my own first hand observations. Those books of a general nature that I have found particularly helpful are listed here, both by way of acknowledgement to their authors and as a recommendation for further reading.

D. M. Anderson, *The Art of Written Forms*, 1969
R. Branner, *Manuscript Painting in Paris during the Reign of St Louis*, 1977
H. Child, *Calligraphy Today*, 1963, 1976
M. T. Clanchy, *From Memory to Written Record: England 1066–1307*, 1979
C. R. Dodwell, *Painting in Europe, 800–1200*, 1971
A. Fairbank and B. Wolpe, *Renaissance Handwriting*, 1960
F. Henry, *The Book of Kells*, 1974
S. Hindman and D. Farquhar, *Pen to Press*, 1977
M. A. Hussein, *The Origins of the Book*, 1970
G. S. Ivy, "The Bibliography of the Manuscript Book", in F. Wormald and C. E. Wrights (eds.), *The English Library before 1700*, 1958
E. Johnston, *Writing and Illuminating, and Lettering*, 1906
N. R. Ker, *English Manuscripts in the Century after the Norman Conquest*, 1960
C. Lawrence, *Fountain Pens*, 1977
E. A. Lowe, *English Uncial*, 1960
E. A. Lowe, *Handwriting*, 1969
R. McLean, *Victorian Book Design and Colour Printing*, 1972
A. C. de la Mare, *The Handwriting of the Italian Humanists*, 1973
A. Martindale, *The Rise of the Artist*, 1972
A. C. Moorhouse, *Writing and the Alphabet*, 1946
F. Mütherich and J. Gaehde, *Carolingian Painting*, 1977
C. Nordenfalk, *Celtic and Anglo-Saxon Painting*, 1977
A. S. Osley, *Scribes and Sources*, 1980
Y. H. Safadi, *Islamic Calligraphy*, 1978
S. H. Steinberg, *Five Hundred Years of Printing*, 1974
D. V. Thompson, *The Craftsman's Handbook*, 1933
D. V. Thompson, *The Materials and Techniques of Medieval Painting*, 1936
J. I. Whalley, *English Handwriting 1540–1853*, 1969
J. I. Whalley, *Writing Implements and Accessories*, 1975

Introduction

A page from the Lindis-
farne Gospels, *c.* 698,
decorated with a goose-
quill pen and ink. Its
delicate artistry and controlled energy can still be
an inspiration to artists
and calligraphers working
now.

I can remember when I was a child, learning to write with a pencil, the
thrill of satisfaction when I finally succeeded in making an egg-shaped O
which actually joined up at the top without missing. I can see that letter
as clearly now as the day I wrote it. Later came the equally exciting
attempts at making real joined-up writing with a dip-pen and red ink. As
I learned to control the pen and to trace coherent words on to the paper I
felt a sense of joy in the making which still remains as vivid in my
memory as the glistening red letters scrawled across the white paper.

On the wall of that schoolroom were pictures of an American Indian
encampment which told their story without written words: this object,
we understood, was a wigwam, and this swaddled baby was a papoose.
Here was the most primitive form of non-verbal story-telling; and in the
same room I learned the rudiments of constructing its descendants—
written letters and words. The story of that evolution is the principal
subject of this book.

The family tree of an alphabet is a reflection of the history of civilisations, marked at every stage by the fortunes of great empires and the
clash of arms. It was the Roman soldiers, not the scholars, who brought
the alphabet to Britain and the rest of Europe; and if Charles Martel had
not beaten back the advancing armies of the Moslem Empire at Poitiers
in 733 AD, this book might well have been printed in Arabic rather than
Roman characters. The administration of nations and empires has
always provided one of the most powerful incentives for changes in the
art of writing and the recording of information.

Yet the story of writing is not only one of the power of conquering
armies or the spread of religions. It was the tools and materials used by
the scribes which gave the letters their form. Every advance in the long
evolution of written forms is related to the limitations and possibilities
of available materials. By learning something of the physical characteristics of these materials—the papyrus sheet and reed brush, the clay
tablet, the stone-carver's chisel, the goose quill pen—we can trace each
step in the story and relive the processes by which change occurred.

That tantalising mixture of frustration and happiness which I remember as a child learning to imitate the letters carefully chalked on the
blackboard may well have been what eventually led me to art college and
to my work as a calligrapher making letters every day. I use traditional
tools—quill pens and reeds—not only because they are still superbly
suited to the purpose of making spontaneous, sensitive and controlled
letters, but because the feel of them in my hands is sympathetic to the
physical and mental act of writing—something a typewriter can never
be. They also exert their own subtle disciplines which draw me in a
physical sense nearer to the letter forms and techniques used by crafts-

lucas uirtulus

on ginned   god spell   æfter   lucas

INCIPIT euangelium   secundum lucam·-

QUO
NIAM

QUIDE
MULTIQ
LIXUNT ORDINA
RENARRATIONEM

men long ago. Some of the most beautifully shaped letters of the Western alphabet were carved into the marble of the Forum in Rome two thousand years ago; but their forms, and the breathtaking workmanship carried on in the monasteries and workshops of medieval Europe, can still provide me with a rich source of inspiration, as I work in the last quarter of the twentieth century.

I realise that I look at this history through English eyes; but I suppose it is as good a vantage point as any from which to look at what happened during the growth and decline of the Roman Empire, and the re-emergence of Christianity that revived the scripts of Rome. Yet our picture of the past, from whatever vantage point, is inevitably limited by what remains have been preserved for us. The earth does not yield up its secrets easily or equally. We have the staggering riches of the Pharaohs' tombs, and the miraculous preservation of Pompeii and Herculaneum, for example, to enlighten us about the life of past ages; but for the most part archaeologists have to make do with chance finds amongst the rubbish tips of past civilisations. They may not always present a true picture: a complicated geometrical theorem written on papyrus would rot away in a few months in damp soil, while a child's sketch of a pig made the same day on a clay tablet might survive intact for five thousand years.

Sometimes the pieces fit together neatly like a jigsaw puzzle, but like the history of most human achievements it is unlikely that the picture was ever a tidy one. The Roman soldiers and administrators brought writing to Western Europe, but after their empire had gradually fallen apart it was Christianity which kept the art alive even during the ravages of the illiterate barbarian tribes. In monasteries established in remote places like the rocky coasts and islands of Britain, the precious Roman texts of the gospels were carefully preserved, and copied out over and over again on to pages of calf or sheepskin.

Despite the violent times, and the dense forest tracks and wild waters of Europe in those days, there must have been a good deal of contact between those remote outposts of literacy. The designs and workmanship of craftsmen and jewellers, goldsmiths and scribes, are proof of the wide-ranging movement of people and the interchange of ideas which took place. How else did the colours of cinnabar, lapis lazuli and ultramarine find their way to places like the windswept island of Iona, where St Columba wrote with ink from the "blue-skinned holly" with a "tired and unsteady hand"? The Emperor Charlemagne may not have been able to write his own name, but his unification of Europe, and the renaissance which followed, eventually gave us the letter form which you are reading now, on this page. He was a Frank living in the eighth century—but his crown was studded with cornelians from classical Rome, and his throne in Aachen was carried there from the islands of Greece. His wife was the daughter of Offa, the English king of Mercia, who may have been illiterate too. At any rate it is unlikely that Offa realised, when he had the design of an Arab dinar copied for his own gold coins, that around his title "Offa Rex" were written the words "Mohammed is the prophet of God" in Kufic script! This wide-ranging

A gold coin of King Offa of Mercia (757–96).

A writing lesson in a London school in 1906. With chalk and slates the children struggle to learn the art of painting speech.

exchange of precious objects of craftsmanship, whether traded or pillaged, must have had a profound effect on the barbarian and early Christian world of visual ideas.

My view of the history of writing is thus illustrated by a series of overlapping pictures, not so much of politics and wars as of things—jewels, caskets, buildings and books—made by hands like yours and mine. The story of writing is told in this book from a calligrapher's point of view; and I believe that anyone who wants to understand this story fully should follow the suggestions and instructions provided for actually making his own pens and his own letters, and feeling for himself the intimate connection between writing tools and materials, and the evolution of letter forms.

When we make things with our hands we put into them energy which comes from our innermost self. When we see and feel objects which were made by craftsmen long dead I believe we can still sense their energy lying beneath each brush-stroke or sweep of the pen, and we can respond to this energy as much as to the object's surface beauty or ingenuity of design. When we ourselves write we not only communicate information by the choice and sequence of the words; we also reveal something of our inner spirit with every tremor of the hand.

So those marks which remain to us from the very beginnings of man's experiments with the alphabet not only provide us with physical evidence of his ingenuity and skill, but like the handwriting of a friend they are an intimate link with his heart and mind. The story of letter-forms is the story of people themselves.

1. The Origins of Writing

Over 30,000 years separate the cave paintings of Lascaux and Altamira in southern Europe from the wall paintings of Egypt. We are no more certain about how the step was made between telling stories with pictures and telling them with symbols than we are about the motives which compelled those early men to draw the magnificent mammoth, reindeer and bison on the walls of their shelters. Their marks were scratched on bones with sharp stones, and drawn and painted on cave walls with charcoal and stick brushes; and they made paint from powdered earth colours mixed with animal fat. Their pictures tell us stories of hunting bison, and of the men who hunted them. We can only say that the instinct to make pictures, which could lead from this world into the world of the mind and beyond, is as deep-rooted as anything we know about our earliest ancestors.

While primitive peoples were continually on the move, following the migrating herds of animals which provided their food, there can have been little chance for them to put down roots or have the leisure to develop anything other than the barest essentials of communication with each other. Only when people became less nomadic, when they learned to cultivate crops and domesticate animals, would the growth of more elaborate language have begun. We can perhaps catch a glimpse of this process when we listen to young children. We can often understand what they are trying to say, long before they can speak properly. A similar simple language no doubt formed a basis of communication between early peoples with their simple range of needs. It is no coincidence, therefore, that the first system of marks which we can call writing has been found in what were once the first arable lands.

As man learned to be a farmer his prosperity and his numbers increased, and so did his need to keep records of transactions, property and religious practices. It is easy to imagine that the simplest way to record the ownership of three cows would be to carve their image on a stone or paint it on a wall; but such records, although durable, would be time-consuming to make. The evolution of pictures into symbols—and from symbols into letters as we know them—must have been driven by the urge for efficiency and utility which is still a driving force of man in our own age. What has made man so successful in the fight for survival is that not only do we adapt to match the changing demands of necessity, but more than other mammals we also enjoy change as an end in itself. Everything we do is subject to fashion, and fashion is nothing if it is not change for its own sake—an expression of the evolutionary, as well as tribal, instincts in us all. We also derive emotional reward from the process of doing and from trying something new, so the answer to one question only leads us to ask another.

A wall painting in the Lascaux caves, dated between 20,000 and 35,000 BC.

Cuneiform

The earliest examples of a writing system of which we have evidence come from the Sumerian settlements of the Fertile Crescent some 5,500 years ago. These remarkable people channelled the waters of the Tigris and Euphrates rivers to irrigate the arid plain on which they settled, and developed one of the world's first advanced civilisations. They built cities, gardens and a flourishing agriculture in a barren desert. They originated the idea of regional government with the centralised distribution of food for the work-force; and cultivated date palms and grew corn. They employed craftsmen in textiles, reeds and leather, as well as doctors, sculptors and engravers. Their civilisation survived from around 3500 BC until it was overthrown some 1,800 years later.

Their writing system, which we call cuneiform, meaning wedge-shaped, provides us not only with a clear picture of the process by which the drawing of simple pictures can evolve into a systematic written language; but also of the influence which the use of certain tools and materials naturally exert on the shape and stylisation of the written forms themselves. Cuneiform script was so successful, moreover, that it was adopted by the Babylonian conquerors of the Sumerian civilisation in 1720 BC, and spread throughout the Semitic nations of the Middle East. And because the Sumerians inscribed their alphabet on tablets of damp clay which were then baked hard, a large number of them have been recovered intact.

Many of the oldest surviving cuneiform tablets are records of temple administration, and provide a glimpse of a prosperous and stable community. They deal with the leasing of land for rent, and the control and recording of labour. In the small city of Lagash, for example, the temple tablets show that within one religious community 48 bakers were employed, as well as 7 slaves, 31 brewers, and spinners, weavers, a smith and other artisans. The Sumerians had not only invented money as a token of value, but lent it to one another at interest. Many of the tablets recovered from temples record the most mundane process of keeping regular and reliable financial accounts. One feature of soft clay as a writing medium is that it does not remain soft for long; and this made it necessary to keep a number of quickly written notes which could be stored until a quantity had been collected, and weekly accounts for instance could then be transferred to a monthly ledger. Thousands of these temporary memoranda have been found in the Sumerian sites.

The temples also provided schools, and pupils' copybooks have survived, with the teacher's writing on one side and the child's imitation of it on the other—and since students and children are the same anywhere far more examples have been found of copybooks which are only half finished than of completed tablets.

With all this evidence available it is possible to trace very clearly the several stages in the development of cuneiform script, and these stages seem to have been the general experience of ancient civilisations—and indeed of primitive people today.

The most embryonic form of writing, as we have seen, is a series of pictures strung together so as to tell a story, leave a message or record information for future reference. The next stage is the reduction and stylisation of such pictures, so that they can be drawn quickly with as few strokes as possible. The Sumerians were especially encouraged to take this second step because of the nature of their writing implements. Although in clay it is quite simple to erase your mistakes, it is not at all easy to create a detailed or elaborate picture.

This stylised symbol of a picture is conventionally known as a *pictogram*. The way in which pictograms come to represent specific objects is not hard to imagine; but concepts like light or day or time cannot be "drawn" in the same way, and new pictograms or old ones were adapted to represent them. The Sumerians thus used the "sun" symbol to stand not only for their word for the sun itself, but for the ideas of "day" and "time". The symbol for an idea is conventionally called an *ideogram*. Today each one of the letters in our Western modern alphabets represents only a separate fragment of sound in most of the words we speak. By repeatedly interchanging these letters, we only need a small family of around thirty shapes to represent every consonant and vowel sound which make up the words of most European languages. The first systems of writing had no such direct connection between symbol and sound.

Ideograms are an efficient means of conveying specific items of information, and are easily and quickly read by everyone (we still use ideograms for international road signs, for example); but for the expression of a series of more complex ideas or of narrative, writing with pictures was unwieldy and the Sumerians had to develop at least 2,000 symbols in order to record and transmit information by this means on to the tablets of clay.

They evidently recognised this disadvantage, and went on to develop the notion that the existing symbol for one object could be extended to represent another object with a similar sound. For example, the pictogram representing a bee could be used to represent any word, or part of a word, in which the sound 'B' occurs. This was a major step, but the adaptation of symbol to sound must have been very gradual, and of course the actual shape of the pictograms evolved and became simplified over the same period of time. These symbols which represent sounds are called *phonograms*, and the combination of two or more phonograms to make up a word we call a *rebus device*. The principle of harnessing sound to a written image was a revolutionary idea, and indeed is still the basis of written language today.

The technique of jabbing into the surface of clay with a sharpened stick, as we have seen, was particularly conducive to simplified symbols and to the process of abstraction; and as soon as a phonogram became established it ceased to be necessary to recognise the picture from which it had descended. This acceptance was helped by the fact that the art of writing in early societies was generally confined to a small number of individuals, and among the Sumerians the priestly caste was able to maintain a tight control over the reservoir of different marks which could be used as pictograms, ideograms and phonograms. This very

Opposite. Stylised pictures gradually evolved into pictograms, in this case for "bird" and "ox", in the distinctive cuneiform style. *Below*. "Bee-leaf". The idea of combining two pictures for their sound value alone, a rebus device, was one of the earliest steps towards a more efficient writing system.

restriction also gave them the power to put into effect the advantages of the phonetic principle, by reducing the 2,000 ideograms and pictograms to a far more practical number – about 600 – of signs, because many of the symbols could be used to "double up" as syllables or parts of words as well as to represent a single object. But the improvement was only relative: there was a long road to travel before a complex language could be written with as few as the 26 letters of our own alphabet.

When the Sumerians were overrun by the Babylonian tribes under King Hamurabai in 1720 BC a considerable part of their culture, including their system of writing and the techniques of the scribes, survived and was adopted by their conquerors. Thousands of Babylonian clay tablets have been recovered, recording religious feasts, history, law, science, mathematics, astronomy and medicine. A number of remarkable texts have been found which confirm and authenticate some of the Old Testament stories. So firmly entrenched was cuneiform writing that its wedge-shapes, deriving from the practical use of a stick in wet clay, were even commonly employed when carving inscriptions into much harder materials like stone. The Babylonian peoples themselves were conquered or assimilated by the Assyrians; and adaptations of cuneiform script spread throughout the civilisations of Mesopotamia – and were adopted by the multiplicity of Semitic tribes of the Middle East.

The flexibility of cuneiform and the principles upon which it was based are underlined by this widespread acceptance among people of all sorts throughout the eastern Mediterranean, and by the variety of purposes for which it was used. Medical texts have been found, for example, which are remarkable for their detail if less convincing as treatment: "purify [and] pulverise the [skin of a] water snake, pour water [over it and] the amamashdubkaskal plant, the root of myrtle, pulverised alkali, barley, powdered fir-resin and the [skin of the] kushippi bird", suggests one of them; and another reads: "pulverise the seed of the carpenter plant, the gum-resin of the markazi plant [and] thyme, dissolve it in beer; let the man drink".

Egyptian Writing

At about the same time as the Sumerians were colonising the lands between the confluence of the Tigris and Euphrates rivers around 3500 BC, a greater and more lasting civilisation had been founded by the Egyptians along the fertile banks of the Nile. The economy of the Egyptians in ancient times was based entirely, as it largely remains today, upon the rise and fall of the Nile flood and the fertility of the alluvial plains along its banks. Almost the earliest inscriptions which survive deal with such matters as the height of the flood, the boundaries of estates (which were always in danger of being washed away by the flood), and the collection of taxes which were linked to the condition of the flooded land. Their government was highly centralised, employing a large number of official scribes, and the development of writing skills could be an essential key to a life of ease and security. In a letter to his son, which was later used for teaching purposes in schools, a high

Egyptian official advised the boy to "love letters like your mother", for through their knowledge "you may protect yourself from hard labour of any kind, and be a magistrate of high repute". Even princes and high officials were fond of having themselves represented in writing postures with papyrus and brush or reading from an opened roll.

Egyptian and Sumerian writing methods developed along similar lines, through the stages of pictogram, ideogram and phonogram; but the Egyptians advanced the process further by creating alphabetical signs. They developed a series of some 24 symbols each representing a single consonant, which provided them with an almost complete working alphabet. Yet they failed for a variety of reasons to take full advantage of the economies made possible by this achievement, and their writing system remained clogged with superfluous signs.

Despite the similar evolutionary stages, Egyptian and Sumerian writing were entirely different in appearance. The first stage, dating from the earliest days of Egyptian literacy, was named *hieroglyphic* (meaning sacred engraved writing) by the Greeks who first saw it some 2,000 years later; and it survived as the writing style appropriate to religious and monumental inscriptions long after the two later stages, known as *hieratic* and *demotic* script had been developed from it. All three styles thus remained essentially picture-writing systems, comprising a combination of pictograms, ideograms and phonograms, even after the simpler principle of alphabetic signs had evolved. The clay tablet had forced the Sumerians and their successors to simplify and improve their system; but Egyptian writing materials ironically may well have had a restraining effect on innovation. Reed brush and ink on papyrus are so fluent and easy to use that there was a less compelling incentive to abbreviate or to discard outmoded forms. Indeed the marriage of liquid

Part of a Sumerian account of fields and crops, from about 2800 BC. The circle represents ten and the semicircular moon shapes represent units.

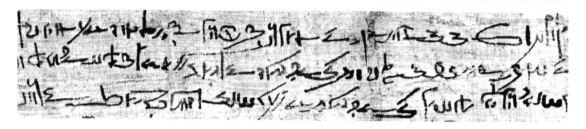

Above. Hieratic writing and, below it, the less formal demotic script which followed. The darker letters clearly show where the scribe had to replenish his pen when it ran dry. *Below.* The traditional hieroglyphs, here carved in stone.

ink, pen and paper first brought about by the Egyptians was such a revolutionary step that it is still the fundamental basis of most hand-written communication today, and the "modern" fibre-tip drawing pen is little more than a machine-produced version of the reed brush.

Up to the 12th Dynasty Egyptian rolls were written in vertical lines from right to left. If the scribe did not stand holding the roll stretched vertically, with the space for his column of writing exposed, he sat with crossed legs and laid the sheet of papyrus across his knees supported by the short kilt which was his traditional dress. The papyrus was thus un-rolled with the left hand and rolled up with the right as the inscription proceeded. After the 12th Dynasty it became the practice to write in short horizontal lines, and the roll was divided up into a succession of narrow vertical columns of horizontal writing. The general practice for short administrative documents, however, was to hold the roll vertically, and to write in longer lines across the full width of the papyrus.

The Egyptians used red ink to indicate titles and headings and the beginnings of new paragraphs. Copyists were careful to try and re-produce as faithfully as possible the works which they were transcribing. The maxims of Ptahhotep which date from the Old Kingdom period were specific on this subject: "Do not leave out a word, do not add one, put none in the place of the other." Sometimes a personal colophon was added, such as that from the *Tale of Sinuhe*: "It has been taken down from beginning to end as it was found written."

The establishment of schools seems to have begun during the period of the Middle Kingdom but before that officials trained young scribes by educating one or more chosen pupils from their own households, and there were "court" schools where the local nobility as well as people from the lower social classes could send their sons to have them educated along with young princes. In these schools the pupil was taught the duties and skills of an official. His intellect had to be sharpened and formed by reading and copying worthy texts, and since the art of oratory was greatly esteemed, attention was paid to the study of rhetoric too. He had to learn the rules and forms of refined letter-writing, as well as the complex, rigid phraseology of oral and written address.

The pupils thus spent many tedious hours copying out model letters and chosen pieces of literature to prepare them for their tasks in the future: "to stand up at the place where there is dispute and to approach the place where there is discussion," where they would be expected to "speak to councillors, to be familiar with the rules at court, to respond to a speech and to send an answer to a letter". Because their writing was not alphabetical but mainly a picture-writing system, the students had to learn and know by heart the hundreds of separate signs, and their precise and orthodox sequence. These hard tasks were not always readily performed by the students and some of them inevitably rebelled; but the teachers were prepared to take drastic reprisals and there are even threats of imprisonment for those who ignored all warnings and threats. If we judge from the texts which have survived, corporal punishment was frequently administered: "do not be lazy for a single day, otherwise you will be beaten. The ear of a boy is on his back, he hears when he is beaten." Yet again the gory details were spelled out: "with the hippopotamus whip I will teach thy legs to idle around the streets!" Even when they were not being beaten or cajoled they seem to have been continually reminded of those harsh alternatives, which they could no doubt see in the streets around them where the hard life of the un-educated peasant and soldier contrasted so unfavourably with that of the scribe and scholar.

The Egyptian brush-pen was made from a thirsty, thin-stemmed rush plant (*Juncus maritimus*), usually cut to a length of around 9 inches. When it is chewed or hammered soft at one end its vascular structure easily frays, and it retains enough ink to sustain the writing of a good number of letters, depending on their size, before it needs recharging. It can be used to draw fine lines, or it can be cut square to produce a letter very like that made by a broad pen nib. The ink used by the Egyptian scribes was so stable that it has retained its dense black colour after thousands of years. It was made of carbon, usually fine soot, mixed with water and a binding agent such as gum. Red ink was made in the same way, prepared with pigment made from one of the many red oxides which occur naturally in the earth. These writing implements, naturally enough, formed the basis of the hieroglyphic sign which was used to represent the word "scribe"; and the bag containing the powdered pigment was often clearly depicted tied with thongs between the brush-holder on the left and the palette on the right, which contained two compartments for red and black ink.

The scribes' tools and methods of working seem to have changed very little over the centuries in Egypt, although in the 5th Dynasty of the Old Kingdom a shell was sometimes used in which to dissolve the ink; and later there is evidence that ready-made cakes of ink similar to the water-colour tablets we can buy today were glued to the upper part of the wooden palette. Its lower part contained a slot in which the narrow reeds were stored when not in use. We can easily reconstruct these materials for ourselves today, and soon discover why they were so

The hieroglyph for "scribe" comprises the traditional palette for inks and a container for brushes, joined to a bag for powdered pigments.

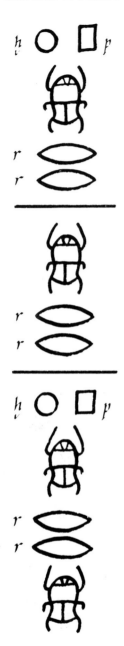

The Egyptians failed to discard the old pictograms even after more efficient alphabetic symbols had been invented.

superbly suited to a writing system that still retained a high proportion of linear picture-drawing among its elements.

In ancient Egypt the tall papyrus plant (*Cyperus papyrus*) grew in still waters all over the country, especially in the marshy districts of Lower Egypt. It was carefully harvested, and its strong fibrous stems were processed and put to use in the making of sails, candles, cloth, cords and mats. There are many wall-paintings in tombs depicting the harvesting of papyrus, although its manufacture for use as a writing material is not shown. However, we can reconstruct the process by closely examining the finished writing material itself. The long, thick, triangular-sectioned stem was first chopped into uniform lengths of about nine inches, and these sections were sliced thinly down their length. The edges of the wafers were then placed side by side longitudinally, each edge slightly overlapping its neighbour. Another layer was then placed at right angles on top of the first, and the whole was hammered and pressed tightly together until they dried in the form of a sheet of writing "paper" held together by the juices in the plant. Any unevenness was smoothed and the edges cut straight, and these separate sheets were glued together with starch paste to form rolls. These might be of any length, but about twenty sheets a roll was usual, and the longest roll known to have survived is as much as 40 metres in length. Papyrus was always an expensive material, partly because its production and sale were subject to royal monopoly from the earliest times. Palimpsests, once-written papyri which were wiped clean and re-used by the scribes, show that economies sometimes had to be made, especially in schools. Limestone fragments and pieces of broken pottery were used as a writing surface for sketches and rough notes, and even these were sometimes washed over and used again. Another surface for occasional note-taking was provided by wooden tablets which had been over-painted with a thin layer of white plaster which could be replaced by another layer when needed. Leather was even more expensive than papyrus and it was reserved for only the most valuable and important texts, such as royal archives or temple rituals.

The large majority of people, obviously, could not read or write; and there is little evidence of any organised "book trade". But at least one standard document seems to have been "published"; even the illiterate seem to have considered it prudent to include a written papyrus among their tomb furnishings, as a passport to guarantee their safe passage to the hereafter, and several of these apparently ready-made documents have been discovered, with the space for the name of the prospective purchaser left open for later insertion.

The Egyptians had all the advantages of 2,000 years or more of stability and continuity, and of convenient writing instruments and materials. Even so, the most efficient phonetic symbols representing single letters which had been developed by at least 1500 BC were often relegated to the simple role of providing additional reassurance alongside the more ancient and cumbersome hieroglyph pictograms. For example, the Egyptian word for beetle was *hprr*, and its pictogram, naturally, was a simple picture of a beetle. But at various stages in the

Papyrus plants grow thickly from the bed of the lake to the left of the hunter, who sails on a papyrus boat.

The scribe-god Thoth records the weight of a human heart against a feather (the symbol of truth). The monster waits to devour the heart if it is found wanting. The figures are drawn with a fine-pointed reed brush, and the hieroglyphs with a square-cut one.

The Egyptian scribe's palette was treasured as an object of status, as well as a working tool.

Making a Reed Pen and a Reed Brush

The reed pen was introduced by the ancient Greeks, and was still favoured as a writing instrument in the West as late as the 16th century. In the East it is still in common use today. Its lightness and pleasant handling qualities make it an ideal pen for expressive calligraphy.

To make a reed brush, take a dried stem of the rush plant (*Juncus maritimus*), and fray the end by chewing it or hammering it.

2. Cut the end at an angle, and make a slit opposite the cut.

4. Slice off the tip at an angle of 60 degrees.

1. To make a reed pen, take the hollow-stemmed reed (*Phragmites communis*), dry and trim it.

3. Shape the nib on either side of the slit, making the two halves match.

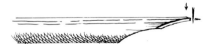

5. Finally, cut the tip square or oblique as required.

Egyptian bureaucracy at work, on a limestone relief from the tomb of Kaninisut, c. 2500 BC. The scribes hold palettes and papyrus rolls, with spare brushes behind their ears, as they listen to dictation. The name of each scribe and his symbol are carved above his head.

development of Egyptian writing we find at least three other versions of writing the word. Each of them still retains the traditional obsolete picture, in addition to the improved alphabetic symbols which should have replaced it. We know that some of the Egyptians must have been aware of the potentialities of the abbreviated system, because they used it when writing foreign names for which they had no traditional hieroglyphic sign; but they did not practise it consistently elsewhere. What had once been an advanced system of written communication stagnated and declined, strangled by its own rigid conventions; and the same might be said of the static condition of Egyptian society itself. The next major improvements in writing systems were developed by Egypt's more energetic and mobile neighbours. The Semitic tribes had devised more efficient and flexible alphabetic techniques suited to the needs of international trade, and in the overlapping variety of systems which emerged from this region we can recognise the beginnings of almost every subsequent writing system used throughout the world today.

2. The Emergence of the Alphabet

There is little simplicity, and even less agreement among scholars, about how the influence and stages of development of the early writing systems were passed on to later civilisations, but most living alphabets are evidently an amalgam of symbols from many sources. The ancient Greeks – according to Herodotus, writing between 484 and 425 BC – believed that their ancestors had acquired the art of letters from the Phoenicians, who, from at least the twelfth century BC, had developed an immensely energetic civilisation based on trading throughout the Mediterranean area, and whose alphabet, based on Canaanite models, had reached maturity at least by 1000 BC. We now know that as early as 3000 BC the beginnings of a writing system existed on the island of Crete, and that by about 2000 BC a phonogram-syllabic script had developed there followed by a second version some 200 years later. Of these two scripts, known as Minoan Linear A and B, only the second has been deciphered; and the language is Greek. It would appear, therefore, that the Greeks possessed a system of writing in the second millennium BC which was lost when the Dorian invaders destroyed their culture around 1100; and that the Phoenician writing system was gradually adopted in Greek lands some three or four hundred years later.

What, then, were the origins of the Phoenician script from which classical Greek writing developed? The Phoenicians were a trading and colonising people based along the coast of Syria, first at Byblos and later at the neighbouring cities of Sidon and Tyre. For over four hundred years from the tenth century they founded settlements westwards throughout the Mediterranean area, along the coast of north Africa, in southern Spain, in Sardinia, Sicily and Cyprus, and on the mainland of Italy and Greece. They exported and traded in cedar and pinewood, fine linen including the famous Tyrian purple (made from a dye squeezed from whelks), embroidery, wine and metalwork; they established an immensely prosperous and energetic commerce throughout the ancient world; and many of their western settlements survived even when Phoenicia itself had been ravaged and conquered by the Assyrians (850–722 BC). With this internationalist outlook the Phoenicians probably built their alphabet from a variety of sources, including cuneiform, Egyptian hieroglyphs, Minoan script and other writing forms that were developing to the north and east of them. In Ugarit one hundred miles to the north of Byblos, for example, an alphabetic writing system using letter-shapes related to Babylonian cuneiform, and with as few as thirty consonantal signs, was in existence before the tenth century. Frequently, they appear to have taken over and simplified the "letters" of other systems and given them new values to reproduce their own consonantal sounds, without necessarily any relation to the original pronunciation.

Relief from the palace of Sargon II (722–705 BC) at Khorsabad, Iraq. Phoenician traders are seen transporting logs along a river.

The physical appearance of the Phoenician script has the "quickly written" characteristics which we might expect from the habitual use of the Egyptian reed brush, but its underlying system was the much more efficient alphabetic one developed by the scribes of the surrounding nations who, because they used the slower manual technique of making records with a wedge stylus in clay, may have been encouraged to develop more simple writing systems. The essential achievements of the Phoenician system were that, unlike the Egyptian, it was self-sufficient and did not require qualification or embellishment with vestiges of an older system; it applied one symbol to one sound, as opposed to one symbol to one syllable; and the symbols were clear and easily written letter-forms which had no pretence to relation to pictures or ideograms. These were the principles, as well as the forms, which the Greeks adopted, absorbed and transmuted, and which also lived on in old Hebrew, Punic and other north African languages. Although the later history of north-western Europe was to take another path, we do know that the Phoenicians sailed as far as the coasts of Brittany and Britain bringing their cultural influences with them, including goods from the exotic and sophisticated cities of Luxor and Salamis. They were men who had seen the pyramids of Egypt and discussed the movements of the

27

heavens with Egyptian astronomers. How did the blue faience beads of Egypt come to be found on Salisbury Plain, or the amber and gold band modelled in the Cretan fashion come into the hands of the people who built Stonehenge? The Minoan burial culture, in which huge quantities of precious objects were buried with the dead and thereby removed permanently from circulation, demanded increasing amounts of gold, silver, tin and lead; and the Phoenician traders who supplied much of these materials were forced further and further afield in search of them. We shall probably never know what elements of Phoenician culture were left behind to be passed on by succeeding generations of the tribes who lived on those remote northern shores.

Eastern Writing Systems

The alphabet developed by the Phoenicians also lies at the root of Eastern writing systems. The Aramaic peoples, of whom the Phoenicians were part, had been settled in Syria before 1000 BC, and had established themselves as prosperous and active traders throughout the area between the Mediterranean and the Euphrates valley. Their writing system was very similar to the one which the Phoenicians spread westwards, including an alphabet more or less identical to it. They were suppressed and dispersed by the Assyrian invasions after 732 BC, but they had already begun to displace the Babylonian language and cuneiform writing with their own throughout the area, and as they moved eastwards this process of linguistic colonisation continued. Aramaic scripts spread throughout the Assyrian Empire, replacing cuneiform systems in the languages of Babylonia and Persia, in the lands around the Persian Gulf, and as far as Afghanistan, India and Mongolia. From these models grew the modern Arabic and Hebrew (Aramaic was the language of Jesus and his contemporaries), as well as the non-Semitic Persian scripts, and the Brahmin script of India; and as recently as the sixth century AD an Aramaic model was used by the Christian St Mashtots as the basis for devising a new alphabet for the Armenian people.

Several references in the Hebrew Bible make it plain that knowledge of writing was taken for granted by the Hebrews at an early date, and in a passage in the Talmud (*Pirqe Aboth*, v. 6) writing and the tools of writing are mentioned among the ten things created on the Sabbath eve in the twilight. And it is widely accepted that an advanced form of alphabetic writing was in common use among Hebrews as well as other Semitic peoples by at least 1000 BC. An alphabet which may well have been the work of a schoolboy has been found scratched into the soft limestone steps of the temple in Lachish, dated about the end of the ninth century. It is written in the conventional order we still use: Aleph, Beth, Gimel, Daleth, He. Once again the unfinished scratchings of a child tell us more than elaborate inscriptions of a more formal nature: by writing out the equivalent of the ABC he provided future generations with the first evidence that the Hebrew alphabet was learned systematically as children do today.

The Arabic script of Islam, which descended from the Nabatean branch of the family of Aramaic scripts, makes its first appearance around 500 AD, but early forms of it had certainly been developed at least two hundred years earlier; and it is not difficult to trace, in its outward shapes at least, not only the Phoenician connection but a direct link with the hieratic and demotic scripts of ancient Egypt. Once this script had been standardised by its use for the writing of the sacred Koran in the early seventh century it was spread by the massive Islamic conquests through north Africa, Asia Minor, and eastwards to India and China. It was only prevented from advancing further throughout western Europe when Charles Martel defeated the Saracen armies at Poitiers in 733 AD.

A Hebrew alphabet scratched into stone, found at Lachish, south-west of Jerusalem, and dated around the end of the 9th century BC.

Chinese Writing

Chinese writing is at least as old as Aramaic, and has survived for 3,000 years as an essentially pictogram-based system. In its early stages it appears to have developed along lines similar to Sumerian cuneiform, proceeding from pictograms to ideograms and to the additional use of phonetic symbols. But the language of China had a peculiar limitation: it consisted almost entirely of single-syllable words. Since there is a limit to the number of possible short sounds the human voice can make (the Chinese use between four and nine hundred), it follows that a large number of these sounds had to share many different meanings. Sounds

A Phoenician alphabetic inscription of the 9th century BC.

with a shared meaning exist in English, of course, such as pear/pare, brake/break or threw/through; in speech we distinguish these so-called *homophones* by their context, and in writing we distinguish them by their spelling. In their language, the Chinese were able to distinguish homophones by the use of four distinct levels of pitch, as well as by the context; but a phonetic alphabet never developed in China because its use would have produced a small number of identically written short words which might have to stand for as many as thirty-eight separate meanings.

In essence the solution reached in Chinese writing was to add an ideogram to each phonogram, to form a composite sign which indicated the context of each of the limited number of sounds. For example, let us take the phonogram for the sound *fang*, which has several meanings including *street* and *inquire*. If we add to the phonogram an ideogram which represents the concept *earth*, we indicate that on this occasion *fang* means *street*. If instead we add the ideogram *words*, we derive the meaning *inquire*. Thus the Chinese developed between two and three thousand separate signs for everyday writing, which with their accompanying ideograms produced a vocabulary of at least 50,000 words.

This writing system was firmly established in China by the first century BC, when a single language was used by all. In the succeeding two thousand years a number of disparate accents, dialects and even separate languages developed or were introduced in China, but the writing system used for them remained common. It is a curious and unique fact, therefore, that people in China who may be unable to converse verbally can nevertheless understand one another in writing. In the same way an American traveller who understands no French can read a timetable in a Paris railway station just as well as a Frenchman. This is because the symbols we use for time – numbers – are pure ideograms common to us all.

fang

earth plus *fang*

words plus *fang*

31

The Greeks

The effect of the so-called Dorian invasions of Greek lands in the twelfth century BC is not easy to reconstruct, and we do not know to what extent the conquered Greek people became assimilated by their invaders, or whether they were entirely driven out. It seems likely that the experience was a catastrophic one, however, since there is archaeological evidence suggesting the wholesale destruction and burning of cities; and the invaders were themselves illiterate. No inscriptions in the Linear B script of the earlier Greek-speaking civilisations have been found after 1200 BC, and the earliest evidence of the arrival of the Phoenician alphabet is dated around 850 BC. In the intervening centuries, we may speculate, isolated Greek-speaking communities survived and slowly recovered their prosperity through contact with the trading activities of neighbouring Mediterranean peoples, and these contacts in due course gave rise to the adoption of an alphabet based on Phoenician models. How and in what form the art of writing survived this dark age will probably never be known.

Minoan "linear A" script, *c.* 1750 BC, which remains undeciphered.

The Phoenician alphabet comprised a limited group of 24 symbols attached to individual consonantal sounds. This range of signs was largely taken over by the Greeks, but it needed substantial adaptation to the requirements of the Greek language, as well as the invention of new symbols particularly for vowel sounds in which the Phoenician, like other Semitic languages, was deficient. A number of variant adaptations of the Phoenician alphabet appeared throughout Greece after 900 BC – almost as many as there were cities – but by 403 BC the so-called Ionic script, as practised in Ionia on the coast of Asia Minor, had become generally adopted and accepted by the Greek city states.

It is a curious feature in the history of writing that early civilisations so often developed systems which were written from right to left (or in vertical columns starting from the right). To our eye and hand this seems both unnatural and inconvenient. A right-handed person – and we have to assume that the majority have been right-handed throughout human history – must, we feel, inevitably find it easier to pull rather than push a writing implement across the surface, and to reveal what he has written as he writes it rather than obscure it behind his hand. Yet the fact remains that most early scripts, including Egyptian hieroglyphs and the hieratic and demotic hands, were predominantly written from right to left.

The practical considerations which may have influenced the change-over are interesting. The soft reed brush will write quite easily, even on the comparatively rough surface of papyrus, in whatever direction it is moved. It is also easy to write with it on a horizontal writing surface, because the absorbent vascular structure of its stem retains the ink and prevents it from flooding onto the paper. The Greeks introduced a new writing instrument, the split-reed pen, which despite its advantages – durability and versatility – brought some new constraints. Cut from one of the hard-skinned, hollow-stemmed species of reed *Phragmytis communis*, not unlike bamboo, and with a point that could be cut square or

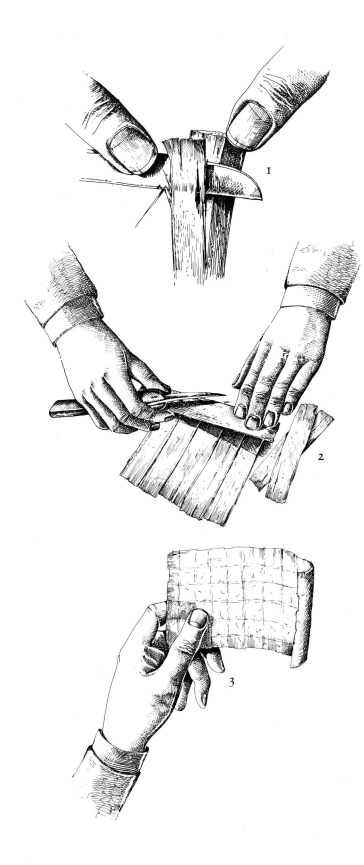

Making Papyrus

In ancient Egypt the papyrus plant had many uses, including the manufacture of boats, sandals and ropes. As a writing material it revolutionised human communications and culture, and after the decline of the Egyptian civilisation continued for more than 2,000 years as the most widely used writing surface in the Western world.

1. Cut away the green outer rind of the plant, and slice thin wafers of the fibrous white pitch down the length of the stem.
2. Lay the wafers alongside each other with edges overlapping. Place a second layer on top of the first, at right angles to it.
3. Hammer the papyrus flat and dry it under pressure. The plant's own moisture contains sufficient adhesive qualities to bind the strips into a strong sheet. After drying, uneven parts can be rubbed and polished out.

The Arabic and Roman alphabets have a common origin.

fine, it stored ink in the hollow tube. On a horizontal writing surface it would easily flood, but to prevent this, to control the flow of ink to the tip, it was natural to tilt the writing surface. Moreover, the hard tip resists being pushed "nose-first" across the rough papyrus page. On an angled board, unlike a surface held horizontally on our knees, our hand obscures the letters to the right of us, and because the space between our body and the writing surface is reduced we have less room for the left-ward movement of the arm. If the letters we have just made are obscured by the hand, it is more difficult to judge their even spacing; and we know from early Greek inscriptions that even spacing was carefully sought after. It is true that in most of the Middle Eastern scripts and Eastern alphabets which developed from them – including Arabic and Hebrew – right-to-left writing has survived. This may be because, although the Egyptians adopted the split-reed pen, they did so at too late a stage for their writing system to be reversed.

The Hebrew scribes continued to write from right to left, but they had traditionally used leather as a writing surface and were among the first to use parchment for the making of records. Both of these surfaces were much smoother and considerably more sympathetic to the harder writing instrument than papyrus. Likewise the widespread use of the Arabic script, after the impetus provided by Mohammed in the sixth century, was first written extensively on animal skins before they were able to benefit as the first importers of fine smooth paper from China. It is interesting to observe, however, that many of the elaborate cursive flourishes which appear at the base of Arabic letters are written by the scribe whilst swinging his pen from left to right, even on the compara-tively smooth surface of paper or vellum.

At first the Greek alphabet followed its Phoenician progenitor in being written from right to left, but it was not long before signs of change occurred, and some inscriptions are even found which show a transition: the lines march from right to left and back again as the plough follows the ox. In the second century BC the split-reed pen was firmly estab-lished, by which time Greek writing was universally left-to-right.

Greek inscriptions engraved in stone or painted on pottery are the earliest to have survived, and they tend to look rigid and geometric. Not surprisingly no examples have been found of writing on papyrus in this period, although it must have been very widespread. The stone inscrip-tions are carefully spaced, deliberate and elegant, but without the free-dom and grace of later handwritten inscriptions – or indeed of the earlier Egyptian hieratic and demotic hands. It seems possible that this early writing style, with its spacious linear angularity, owed much to the common use for day-to-day note-taking of another writing material: the wax tablet. This comprised a wooden base, rebated with raised edges, and the hollow filled with a sheet of wax on which letters could be scratched with an iron or wooden stylus. The tablet could be erased by using the handle of the stylus to polish out the letters; the friction of rapid rubbing melts the wax slightly, and smooths the waxen surface for re-use. Like the clay tablets of the Sumerians, this method encourages the adoption of straight lines and thus perhaps of angular letters.

Detail from a Greek vase of 540 BC. Achilles' and his opponent's names read from left to right, but the inscription on the left is written in the other direction.

Unglazed pieces of pottery were also used for writing on by the Greeks, as they had been by the Egyptians, and many such pieces of so-called *ostraca* have survived from all periods. The name derives from the practice of the advisory council in Athens of holding secret ballots from time to time to decide upon the names of those citizens who were regarded as being too powerful or in some respect dangerous to the *demos*. Names were written on an *ostracon* and placed in an urn. If anyone received too many votes he was ostracised: condemned to banishment from Athens for ten years.

To begin with the scribe writing literary works on papyrus with a reed pen made similar letter forms to those used for inscriptions in stone or pottery. Gradually, by the end of the fifth century BC, the separately formed capital (or majuscule) letters gave way to more fluently written rounded forms, and in addition to the formal styles used for literary works, cursive scripts in various styles were developed, which being easier and quicker to write could be used for everyday or informal purposes, for business transactions and to record the activities of a growing bureaucracy.

Papyrus, as we have seen, had been the natural writing surface for the Egyptians, and it was exported for the use of scribes throughout the Mediterranean world. It had been a highly profitable state monopoly in Egypt from at least 3000 BC, and for almost 4,000 years its use dominated the cultural life of every civilisation that came in contact with Egypt. But by the second century BC the needs of the rising Roman Empire were added to those of the Greeks, and shortages occurred which led to an increase in the price of papyrus. An alternative was sought. Pliny the Elder reports the tradition that the invention of parchment or writing skin was the outcome of a rivalry between Eumenes II of Pergamon in Asia Minor and Ptolemy of Egypt between 197 and 158 BC, over the growing reputation of Pergamon as a centre of scholarship. The jealous Ptolemy, it is said, cut off the supplies of papyrus upon which Eumenes' scribes depended, and he was forced to seek alternatives. To this day the word parchment reminds us of Pergamon's claim to have invented it.

In fact, the skins of animals had been used for writing from very early times – examples survive from Egypt around 2500 BC – but no doubt the growing needs of new civilisations forced an improvement in the techniques of curing and preparing them. Leather is highly durable, and can be attractive in appearance. The Dead Sea Scrolls, found by accident in the desert of Judaea in 1947, are probably the most famous leather documents to have survived from ancient times. Leather still plays an important part in the Jewish ritual: a book of laws must at all times be written on skin, even today, and all synagogues have their leather or parchment "torah" scrolls. Nevertheless, documents made of almost any material wear out after continual use, and this is recognised by the custom which the Jewish scholars and priests observed. They revered each sacred book so highly that even when it was worn out they did not discard it but carefully locked it away in a special store which was called the Genizah.

Sheep, cattle and goatskins were normally used, but writing has been found on the skins of gazelle, antelope, stags and even ostriches. One side of leather only – the hair side – could be used; and if the tanning was imperfect it could also be unpleasant to handle and give off an extremely pungent smell. Al-Baladhuri reports how the Sasanian king Khusrau Parves was so irritated by this disagreeable effect that he gave orders that in future all annual tax rolls should be stained yellow with saffron

A Greek inscription of 340 BC. We still use all but four of these characters today.

Greek writing on a wax tablet, from 4th- to 5th-century Alexandria. The inscription reads "the true beginning of life is writing", and is evidently an exemplar to be copied by a student.

and sprinkled with rose-water.

True parchment is made from sheepskin. It is first steeped in lime, and the hair and flesh are carefully scraped from the surface before it is stretched tight over a frame, covered with chalk to remove excess fats, and allowed to dry. After further scraping with a moon-shaped blade, while still on the frame, the skin is then removed and cut to size. Both sides can be used for writing. Vellum, made from calfskin, was similarly prepared; and in general terminology all writing skins are still referred to as parchments. They have an advantage over leather which was usable on one side only, and are more durable for prolonged use than the fragile papyrus. Nonetheless it took several hundred years before parchment began to rival papyrus in the Roman world, where as late as 273 AD the Roman pretender, Firmus Brutus, could still boast that an entire army could be equipped and supported on the revenues from the papyrus trade alone. As we shall see, the eventual adoption of parchment as the universal writing surface had a profound influence on the invention of the codex, as opposed to scroll, form of the book. Meanwhile, whether the Greeks of Pergamon get credit or not for the refinement of parchment-making techniques, they and their contemporaries nonetheless continued to rely substantially upon papyrus for everyday writing use throughout the Greek and Roman worlds.

3. Rome

Either through Etruscan influence or by direct contact with the Greeks, the early Roman people assimilated and adapted the Greek alphabet. The letters A B E Z I K M N O T X and Y were taken over with hardly any change; Greek symbols were remodelled and adapted to make the letters C G L S P R and D; and the letters V F and Q were taken from Greek letters which had become obsolete in the Greek language. After their early beginnings both Greek and Latin carved inscriptions began to show increasing confidence and elegance in both design and execution. It is fair to assume that at least by the third century BC both Greek and Roman scribes were also in possession of a cursive (quickly written) alphabet developed from the more formal shapes of the capital letters. When Greece became part of the Roman Empire after 146 BC, Greek survived as the language of scholarship throughout that empire, as well as in Greek-speaking lands—notably Egypt where Greek continued as the official language of the civil service.

By the end of the second century BC, when their empire had already reached eastern Spain, north Africa and parts of Gaul, the Romans had developed a complete family of alphabets, answering the needs of every aspect of life. At the head of the group is the majestic and aptly named *capitalis monumentalis*, and alongside it the narrower and more condensed form of the *capitalis rustica*. The finer points of the serifs (the cross-line finishes of each stroke) of both letter forms are intimately connected with the physical process of carving them in stone with a chisel, for which purpose they were essentially designed. And the thick and thin strokes of the letters themselves owed much to the chisel-shaped brush and square-cut reed pen.

Letter-carving in stone was always preceded by careful planning, since not even the most expert stone-carver could contemplate beginning to cut into the smooth stone of an important monument or building before the whole inscription had been carefully laid out. The dimension of the stone and the number and relative importance of the words of the inscription unavoidably dictated the size of the letters and their relationship with each other and the surrounding space. The height of the letters and the space between the lines are not only dictated by the height of the stone, but also by the width, since tall letters give a longer line than the same number of small ones. Within these limitations the designer juggled the words into some sort of visual as well as literal sense, very probably drafting out his ideas on a large roll of papyrus. Once this arrangement of size and number of lines was sketched, the inscription could be set out on to the stone. Lines would be "snapped" across to indicate the top and bottom of the letters, no doubt just as a signwriter does today: by holding a chalk-loaded line taut from one side of the

stone to the other, plucking it away and letting it snap back to leave perfectly straight chalk dust lines of uniform thinness between which the letter painter could indicate with chalk or charcoal pencil the shape and position of each letter which had been decided beforehand. Letters could then be painted with confidence over the rough drawing without fear of overrunning the edges of the stone. The chisel would follow the rounded and fluent curves of the brush-strokes, and the letters frequently show the marked gradations from thick to thin which were naturally made by the chisel-edged brush as it turned. This gradation did not occur with Greek letters, but the Roman predilection for regularity and precision in all things did lead them to adopt the Greek rule of basing the formal *capitalis monumentalis* on a geometrical framework of squares, the circles which fit within them and half-squares of regular size. In practice, however, the letter-shapes do not always conform easily to these rules, and the letters and spaces between them were ultimately a matter for the judgement of the eye.

Many of the individual forms, as we have seen, are drawn from a wide variety of sources far back into distant antiquity, and letters like A which descended from the shape of an ox's head, and N from the hieroglyph for snake, did not always submit meekly to geometric conformity with more recent upstarts like X and Q. Even in the best regulated inscriptions the letter R often strides defiantly outside its invisible half-square, as if anxious to get on with the story. The top half of the well-fed and well-bred letter B invariably follows slightly behind its rotund "belly", and

Formal inscriptions on tombs and monuments required careful planning. The long text carved on this monument on the Appian Way near Rome must have been roughly sketched several times in order to get the letters to fit the shape of the stone.

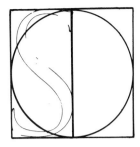

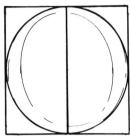

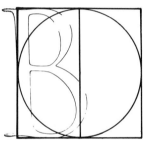

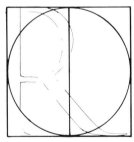

The *capitalis monumentalis* alphabet, a Roman inscription from the 1st century AD. No doubt compasses and straight edges were used to make the framework of squares, half-squares and circles which underlie the shapes of these letters; yet the designer has subtly rebelled against this geometric regimentation, and the letters take on a personality of their own.

the top of the rounded C and G would appear to wilt if they did not refuse to bow their heads beneath the invisible roof delineated by the unfeeling compasses.

By drawing a line along the top of an inscription we discover that the designers also consciously pushed some letters, like the pointed A and rounded O and C, above it. This was because they understood the need to compensate for a visual weakness of these letters. Being tapered at their tops, they make less visual impact than their neighbours with square tops on the invisible ceiling which our eye unconsciously draws along the line as we read.

It has often been noted that it is the use of space – letter-spacing, word-spacing and line-spacing – which distinguishes the finest inscriptions, and the Roman letter-carvers appear to have recognised that there are no mathematical or geometrical rules that can be applied to this art. There were of course variations on these methods. Some inscriptions definitely were drawn out with geometrical instruments directly on to the stone, for the marks of the compass points still remain in the centres of the rounded letters, as do scratched guidelines. But whatever method was used, a great number of the formal inscriptions on Roman buildings all over the empire which we admire to this day combine consciously sophisticated design with fine aesthetic judgement, and they were always the result of careful planning: stone does not readily forgive mistakes.

The *capitalis monumentalis* and *rustica* alphabets were widely used for inscriptions carved into stone or painted onto walls, as temporary notices, election posters for example; and both alphabets are frequently found written in ink with a reed pen on papyrus or ostraca. The slowly-formed individual capital letters of these alphabets were never ideally suited to accurate imitation in quickly written form, even though books do exist as late as the fifth century AD where the quadrata (or square Roman letter) as well as rustic forms have been carefully reconstructed with a pen on vellum; but they were rare, luxury volumes. In addition the Romans had, like the Greeks, developed a quickly written capital letter, the Roman cursive majuscule, as well as a diminutive version with looping joins above and below the writing line – not dissimilar in essence and function to the hasty ball-point scribble of modern times. Both these variants grew out of the need for a practical and speedy writing system for daily use. By the first century AD all these writing styles had become universal throughout the entire Roman Empire, from the Euphrates to the northernmost boundary in Britain.

Rome was now the hub of the largest empire the world had ever known, and in this administrative centre there must have been plenty of work for the professional scribes and carvers: in the chanceries administering the government of the empire, in the counting-houses of the merchants who imported and exported goods through the port of Ostia, in the streets writing letters to order, and in the production of the vast number of monumental inscriptions with which Rome was filled. The Roman imperial chancery (or office of letters) was divided into Greek and Latin departments; and in later centuries we know that it had developed into a number of specialised sections: the letter office for

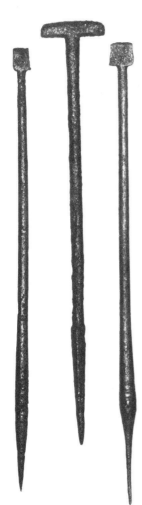

foreign, legal and administrative affairs; the petition office, for petitions and investigations; the memorandum office, for short decrees; and an office for general internal administration. By the fourth century a group of notaries also provided personal secretaries for the Emperor. The functions of writing varied enormously and the standards set by the scribes differed accordingly. In the edicts of the Emperor Diocletian in 301 separate maximum prices were set for the writing of a hundred lines of text, in documentary, first- and second-class book hands.

A high proportion of the Roman citizenry was literate even in the time of the Emperor Augustus (63 BC to 14 AD), but for the most part everyday copying was apparently delegated to slaves. The production of a book in several editions was carried out by the simple expedient of having a number of scribes (often but not always slaves) writing together in one room, dictated to by the author or by a reader.

Roman writing and culture travelled with the army to every corner of the Roman world. The Emperor Claudius with four legions had conquered Britain in 43 AD, but it proved a very expensive and unstable conquest, for in the three hundred years that followed there were never less than three legions on British soil. Spain, on the other hand, which had taken much longer to subdue, had thereafter required a Roman garrison only one legion strong to maintain order. Britain was a remote and savage place, and the Caledonians to the north and the Celts to the west always remained outside Roman control. Because so many troops were present in Britain throughout the Roman period we are left with a remarkably rich picture, through archaeological remains and literary references, of what life was like in this outpost of the empire.

In Roman society a career in the army was widely regarded as providing the best possible preparation for the life of a magistrate, politician, poet or historian, and many young men of Roman citizenship would have performed at least some military service overseas. A legion was

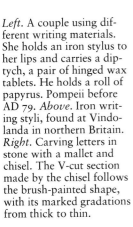

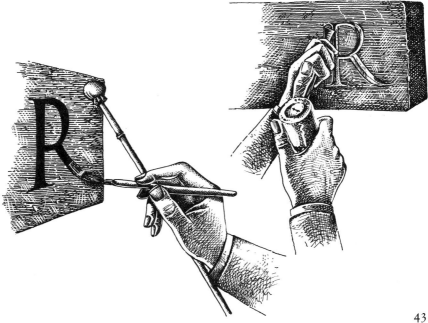

Left. A couple using different writing materials. She holds an iron stylus to her lips and carries a diptych, a pair of hinged wax tablets. He holds a roll of papyrus. Pompeii before AD 79. *Above.* Iron writing styli, found at Vindolanda in northern Britain. *Right.* Carving letters in stone with a mallet and chisel. The V-cut section made by the chisel follows the brush-painted shape, with its marked gradations from thick to thin.

about 6,000 strong, including officers as well as non-combatant staff (orderlies, clerks, priests, doctors, engineers and surveyors), and commanded by an officer of senatorial rank, the highest social class. It was clearly a standing joke in smart Roman circles to grumble about the hardships of such service: as the poet Florus wrote, *Ego nolo Caesar esse ambulare per Britannis* ("I should not like to be Caesar, touring Britain"). The legions formed the back-bone of the army, but they were supported by auxiliary units of non-Roman citizens from every part of the empire. The soldiers of the 2nd Cohort of Hanii, who came from the mountains of Yugoslavia, would no doubt have worried less than the Romans about the weather in northern Britain, although it would have been less congenial to the archers from Syria. All these forces, and many others, have left signs of their presence on Hadrian's 80-mile-long Wall, completed in 117 AD to keep out the savage tribes to the north of it.

The protection provided by the wall and the presence of such a substantial army created thriving townships in northern Britain which attracted traders from all over the Roman world. From Britain they exported corn, cattle, hides, gold, silver and iron, as well as slaves, "clever" hunting dogs, oysters and even bears, which were transported to provide a spectacle in the arenas of Rome. British soldiers in their thousands fought alongside the Roman legions throughout the empire.

Along the wall the soldiers who built each section left their cohort's signature inscribed in rough letters into the stone with an iron chisel; and elsewhere more expert craftsmen carved elegant inscriptions over

Wedge feet created by the chisel brush are imitated by the iron chisel of the Roman carver.

the porticos of temples, dedications to gods or emperors, and memorials to a wife, a child or a friend. Many of them are elegant enough to have graced the walls of Rome itself. One tombstone found by the wall is that of a surgeon, another of a slave. A certain Barates, who may have been a standard-bearer, left a memorial to his wife inscribed in both Latin and in the Palmyrian script of his native Phoenicia.

A great deal of less formal writing must have been done in these cosmopolitan communities of the Roman Empire, much as it was in Rome itself: personal correspondence, local administration, and the reports and despatches of the garrison commanders to their superiors. Writing instruments such as iron styli for writing on wax tablets, "unspillable" inkpots made of Samian ware, and even metal pens have been discovered in settlements south of Hadrian's Wall. At Vindolanda examples have been found of letters written on thin slivers of wood, one of which is from a soldier to a friend or relative at home, listing food and other provisions which he wants sent out: two pairs of sandals, woollen socks or felt slippers, and two pairs of underpants.

The appearance of the book as we know it, the codex form of folded pages gathered and sewn together, seems to have coincided with the spread of Christianity. Certainly the earliest complete Greek book which survives, the *Codex Sinaiticus*, is a Christian Bible of around the fourth century. There are earlier fragments of Roman secular books, too, but the success of the book as opposed to the traditional roll form was just as much practical as cultural. It was never easy to refer to specific sections in long passages of text written on a roll. Only one side of the papyrus was written on, because the reverse had to be handled constantly as it was rolled and unrolled; and papyrus was expensive.

Parchment, too, was expensive, as we have seen, but because of its

1st-century AD graffiti painted on a wall at Pompeii, announcing gladiatorial contests and elections. The larger letters are a narrower form of the *capitalis monumentalis*. Below, when the brush is held at a steeper angle it creates the thin downstrokes and heavy feet of the *rustica* style.

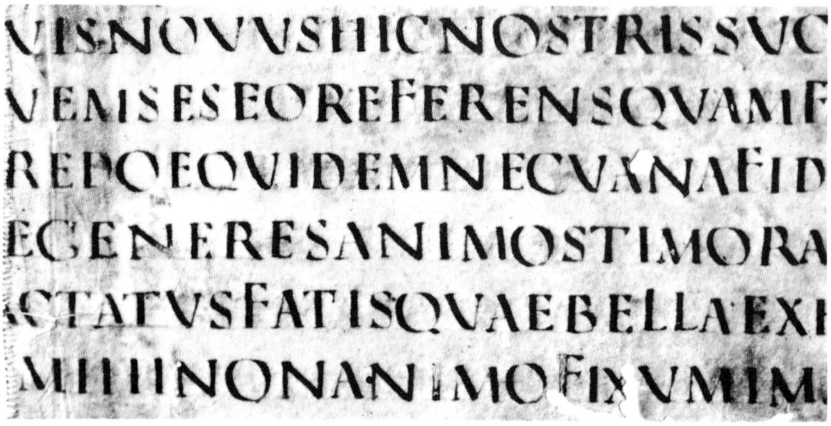

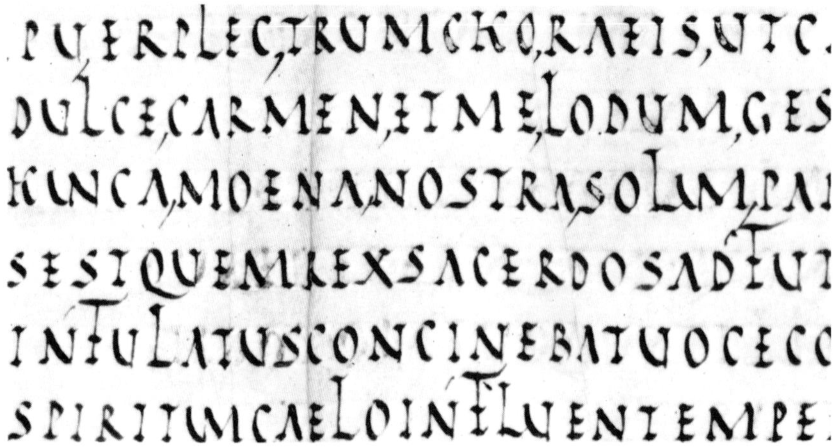

VIS NOVVS HIC NOSTRIS SVC
VENIS ES EO REFERENS QVAM F
REPO EQVIDEM NEC VANA FID
EGENERE SANIMO STIMORA
ACTATVS FATISQVAE BELLA EXI
MIHI INONAN IMO FIX VMIM

PVER PLECTRVM CKORATIS UTC.
DVLCE CARMEN ITMELODVM GES
HVNC AMOENA NOSTRA SOLVM PAI
SES IQVEM REX SACERDOS ADIVI
INIVLATVS CONCINEBATVOCECC
SPIRITVM CAELO INILVENI EMPE.

Left. Pen-made square capital letters on vellum, 5th-century. Below. Rustic letters written with a quill on vellum, probably 6th-century. Writing skins were capable of sustaining a much finer line than the rough surface of papyrus. Both these late Roman examples show how the sharply cut pen on vellum could be made to reconstruct the carved and painted shapes of formal inscriptions. Right. Hadrian's Wall, built around 117 AD. Gangmarks were roughly inscribed with iron chisels on the wall after each cohort finished building its section, recording its number and the name of its commander.

resilient fibrous composition a sheet could be folded in a sharp crease without cracking along the fold, and when folded sheets were sewn together only the two exposed sides of the outer leaves were needed to protect the rest.

There were, of course, some intermediate experiments. Composite books have been found, made of both parchment and papyrus; and some of the early methods of book construction seem to be related to those used to hinge wax writing tablets which were folded in a concertina fashion. However, the simple codex idea displaced all others, and in 1,700 years it has not been improved upon as a private, trouble-free and portable "information retrieval system".

Before the widespread adoption of writing skins along with the codex book, there would have been little incentive to develop a more refined form of writing instrument than the reed pen, since the rough surface of papyrus was not conducive to fine, small writing. Parchment or vellum, however, being smoother, may well have encouraged the development and popularity of the quill pen made from the strong flight feathers of a goose or similar large bird. The composition of a quill is not unlike human fingernail; it is tougher than the split reed, and can write small letters finely for long periods without re-sharpening. Since the barrel of a

46

This wooden tablet was discovered at Vindolanda, three miles south of Hadrian's Wall. Notice how the split-reed or quill opened as pressure was applied and the ink gave out, leaving characteristic pen-written marks.

quill was entirely similar in principle to the hollow reed, the scribes needed to make only minor adaptations of their traditional methods when shaping it for writing.

In the later history of Roman civilisation the crucial event in the story of writing was the adoption of Christianity as the official religion of the Empire in 313 AD; for it was primarily through the Christian churches and monasteries that the art of writing was preserved throughout Europe when the Empire began to fall apart. The monastic tradition particularly, which had begun as early as the fourth century as a protest against the worldliness of the Church no less than of the world itself, made an immense contribution to the preservation and advancement of

IRANSUNTETRE· PACIT
CERUNTOMNIA [XIX· ANNOCC
IXEO· qu·
TPLACUITSERMO moe
INCONSPECTURE EXIITO

dicifarinacoctuminydreleo etpanerant
multiturcumrucocrambirhaechiniu
unt· Inautemcalidapodagra adhiber
madehordeifarina cumoleocammelo
enrimulcoctum· Mittatetprilliain
quacalida iubatmirabiliter· FINITDOGRATIAS·

the written word. Uncial and half-uncial scripts were the main book hands used in the late Roman period: they had none of the hauteur or erect martial bearing which characterised the carved inscriptions of more confident times, nor were they related to the cursive vernacular scripts which enjoyed a vigorous plebeian life of their own. It was the comfortable, rounded and mellow shapes of these formal uncial and half-uncial letters which were used by the Christian scribes to copy and recopy the Bible, gospel books and teachings of the early church fathers.

The Roman instinct for organisation was inherited by the Western Church, and monasticism became a pioneering force, evangelising among the tribes of northern and western Europe. When by 476 the line of Roman emperors in the West had ended, many of the barbarian tribes who supplanted them throughout southern Europe were already Christian; and the monkish missionaries continued to push their way through Gaul into the far north. Celtic monasticism, especially from Ireland, played a leading role in the advance. And in the shapes of the letters written by Irish monks in their remote havens, copying and illuminating the gospels, we can trace a clear descent from the uncial scripts of the Roman gospels.

Two book hands of the late Roman Empire: full rounded letters, later known as uncial (6th century); and below, the half-uncial, with ascenders and descenders (6th to 7th centuries). The latter might have formed the basis for the minuscule scripts developed in Irish and other outlying Christian centres. They have a rotund strength, but no longer reflect the grandeur of imperial Rome.

49

4. Writing in the Dark Ages

Opposite. A page from the *Book of Kells*, around 700 AD. Despite its complex appearance the basic components are simple. Compasses and rulers were used to create the framework of the designs, which were then filled with pen-drawn detail and laid in with colours.

Irish Christianity was traditionally founded by St Patrick, a genuine Roman Briton whose father was a Roman citizen and a Christian. From about 400 AD monasticism took root in Ireland, and it proved fertile soil: perhaps because of the similarity between the "family" organisation of the monastery and the traditional Celtic concept of a clan-based tribal society. Although the Irish Church was cut off from the Christian centres of mainland Europe, the sea routes remained open linking it with the Mediterranean world; and we know that wine, fine pottery and amphorae from north Africa – perhaps accompanied by knowledge of the intensely pious and ascetic tradition of monasticism in Egypt and the East—found their way to Ireland and to the other monastic settlements along the Atlantic seaboard, in Spain, Aquitaine, western Britain and Scotland.

For the Irish scribes, who no doubt at first made only stumbling copies of the precious manuscripts and gospels of Rome, there were soon many other influences in the air. The painting with which they decorated their work had reached high levels of artistry, and shows all the vigour and fierceness—snarling beasts, coiling snakes—which the heathen Saxons displayed in their jewellery. As the Romano-British people began to be driven westwards into Ireland by the invasions from northern Europe, their craftsmen took with them techniques and designs learned from the invaders. The Irish scribes must have found them compelling, for their manuscripts begin to sing with vibrant colour and writhe with the vivid imagery of Germanic animal ornament, interwoven in continuous chains and laces around the page. At the same time their work retains an essentially Celtic sense of mystery and respect for the older gods, for the ancient magic of their own past. The letter-shapes even seem closer, sometimes, to the mysterious talismanic symbols of the ancient Teutonic runes than to the rotundity of Roman book script. Finally, there is another cultural element woven into these manuscripts—a striking similarity to oriental illumination and to the textile designs of Coptic Egypt and Islam. It reminds us that in those long years when Ireland was cut off from much of Europe, Egypt and the Eastern monastic tradition must have seemed closer than Rome. And in their isolation the island scribes were free gradually to modify the majuscule book scripts which they had inherited from the Roman world: like a story whispered around a crowded room, what eventually emerged was distinctly different from the original—the Irish half-uncial script of the *Book of Kells*. Out of the majuscule, half-uncial letters they also created the first formal minuscule (what we now call "lower case") alphabets—not quickly scribbled cursive versions of capital letters, but a separate family of well-developed small letters in their own right.

The *Book of Kells* as we know it today is, alas, only a shadow of its former self. Despite the depredations of time and of the attentions of successive restorers and rebinders* it still stuns the eye with its throbbing colours, and warms the mind with the energy it contains and releases. This was precisely the effect it was designed to create, as an altar-book for liturgical reading and for display. It is in many ways a typical example of the work of the Insular (Irish-British) school of scribes in the seventh and eighth centuries, although it was produced by a number of different artists and scribes over several decades and possibly in different places. It is important, however, not to confuse the length of time which may have elapsed between the start of a project like the *Book of Kells* and the date when work finally stopped with the amount of time spent actually working on the pages. No monk, let alone a competent professional lay scribe, ever spent a lifetime copying a single page. There is no doubt that then, as always, speed harnessed to skill was the vital ingredient in the execution of such work, allowing the scribe to maintain rhythm and harmony in the writing and freshness and life in the drawing.

Since the beginning of Christianity parchment (the skins of calf and sheep), had steadily displaced the use of papyrus as a writing material in the West. This is almost certainly due to the fact that the strong, thin and flexible membranes were so ideally suited to the hinged codex form of book; but as we have seen parchment has another characteristic which had a profound effect on the style and detail of the decoration and writing of manuscripts like the *Book of Kells*. The surface of the writing skin after it has been scraped has a smoother and more even surface than papyrus ever had. The combination of this surface with the fine but relatively tough quill pen created new technical possibilities for the artists of the Dark Ages which had not been utilised by the scribes who had worked with the coarser materials of the reed pen or brush on papyrus.

After the skins had been scraped and smoothed, leaving a slight velvety nap on the surface, the pages would be cut and collected into gatherings of four or more sheets. These would then be folded down the centre, and pricked through the several thicknesses in accordance with a measured grid to provide the framework of the design and to indicate the position of lines for writing. The pages would then be unfolded to reveal exactly identical marks on both right- and left-hand sheets (recto and verso), and the pages would be ruled by scoring with a smooth hard point leaving an indentation on one side of the skin and a raised line on the other, thus obviating the need to rule both sides.

The basic designs used by the scribes were not invented afresh, but inspired by previous work, copied, adapted and combined. As the scribe worked he would have access to other manuscripts containing a great many of the ideas which we see in the *Book of Kells*. A well established

---

*Such butchery still goes on, in ill-directed "conservation" programmes in museums throughout the world. Museums have two functions: (a) to make their collections available for study; and (b) to conserve them. In the case of books the two functions inevitably conflict. Books wear out through use and careless handling; but far more damage is done to them every day through insensitive and often unnecessary restoration.

The monastery of Skellig Michael, perched on a rock 600 feet above the Irish Sea. It was in places like this that Christianity, and with it the art of writing, was kept alive after the Roman Empire declined.

community such as Iona, for instance, might well have had in its library Roman, Coptic, Syriac, Armenian and Byzantine manuscripts which had been collected over a long period, their intricacy, richness and ingenuity already the product of a long evolution.

The chosen design was first faintly scored on the page, probably with a silver-point or stylus (the pencil as we know it did not then exist), and over these marks more detailed drawings would be made onto the skin with a fine quill pen and very pale ink. Compasses were used to draw circles, and straight-edges and set-squares were also employed for straight lines and angles. The Celtic craftsmen may well have had the ability to make adjustable metal pens similar to those we still use for the drawing of fine, straight, mechanically even lines in ink. But it would be a mistake to look for mechanical explanations before giving credit to the supreme technical skill of these ancient scribes in their preparation and use of the quill pen. Art historians often seem to look to mechanical aids to explain away what may seem to them superhuman skill, but a pen made from the flight feather of a crow is capable of producing very fine lines indeed and even the square-cut goose quill when held at an angle to the surface so that it writes on a "corner" of its nib produces a monoline of uniform weight.

With the design faintly penned out, the colour was then laid in for the most part still using a quill pen because of its effectiveness on the surface of the skin. It is as difficult to paint fine lines with a brush on a velvety surface as it would be to do so on a carpet. A pen, however, forces the "pile" down and creates a narrow groove into which the ink will flow and remain contained, producing much finer lines than we are used to creating on the shiny surface of modern paper. Once the edges of the colour had been drawn with the pen, however, the scribe would fill in the larger coloured areas with a brush, a fine-haired one perhaps made from the fur of the pine marten. Manuscripts in the later Middle Ages often contain fine white highlights painted in white lead paint; but this technique seems to have been little used in the *Book of Kells*, or at any rate very little of it remains. Instead the artists frequently made use of the vellum background to achieve the same effect, so that brilliance was often imparted by leaving tiny white spaces unpainted, to peep through the outlines and colour and give zest to the design.

Although the *Book of Kells* is so full of brilliant colour it is a surprise to find that it contains not a single scrap of gold. What many people, seeing reproductions of the book, take to be gold-leaf decoration is in fact achieved by the lavish use of orpiment (arsenic trisulphide). In its natural state orpiment has a mica-like sparkle which has the appearance of metallic gold, which tormented medieval alchemists so much that for generations they tried unsuccessfully to extract gold from it. Orpiment was imported from Asia Minor, and although its brilliance is undeniable its use creates great problems for the illuminator. The sulphur content "attacks" the neighbouring colours. But examining the book, one can see that the illuminators understood these chemical properties perfectly: often the orpiment yellow is carefully painted within protective boundaries of a brown ink line or of unpainted vellum, preventing it from coming into contact with other colours. On some occasions they have even succeeded in drawing other colours over it with no ill effect.

Orpiment can also have a corrosive effect on the colour-binding materials used, and the makers of the *Book of Kells* were less successful in preventing this occurrence: in places the yellow has decayed and cracked away from the surface.

It is still uncertain whether the brilliant blues in the *Book of Kells* are made from ultramarine or from azurite, and the procurement of either

would have caused formidable problems for the Irish scribes. Ultra-marine was the most rare and valuable pigment in existence, whose only known sources were Persia and Afghanistan. It was acquired from these remote regions by Arab traders, processed in the Middle East, and sold for enormous prices. More than four hundred years were to pass before the secret of its manufacture – it was made by grinding the semi-precious stone lapis lazuli – became generally known in Europe. Azurite, the carbonate of copper, could be obtained nearer at hand, from the copper deposits on the mainland of Scotland and in northern England; but if this was used we have to assume that the technology of refining it was available – which is by no means certain. A final solution to this question awaits a full chemical analysis of the colours of the *Book of Kells*.

Another colour used plentifully throughout this ancient book is verdigris (cupric acetate), with its cold green hue. This unstable colour has an alarming habit of corroding the parchment, eating through it so that nothing but gaps are left on the page where it was painted. Cennino Cennini in the fourteenth century thought it "very lovely to the eye", but "it does not last". Yet in the *Book of Kells* it has behaved quietly and stayed in place for over 1,200 years.

Other pigments used by the Irish scribes also had to be imported, such as kermes, an insect dye from which a crimson colour was made. They may have used the woad plant to make a violet-blue colour instead of imported indigo, and they made pigments from white and red lead. Vegetable and animal extracts were both made to produce transparent dyes.

It is certain, therefore, that fine colours were imported from far afield to the island monasteries, places that even by today's standards are

A Saxon purse lid, orna-mented in cloisonné enamel, garnets and mille-fiore. The designs of the *Book of Kells* echo the pagan enameller's tech-nique. Sutton Hoo trea-sure, 7th century.

Cutting a Quill Pen

A sharp knife and patient practice are needed. Select the feather from one of the first five flight feathers of any large bird, such as a goose. Feathers from the left wing fit the right hand best. Soak the feather until it is soft, then harden it in hot sand. Proceed as follows:

1. Having shortened the plume, strip away the barb, which would otherwise rest uncomfortably against the knuckle of the index finger.

2. Cut away the tip of the barrel at an angle.

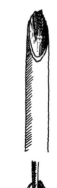

3. Make a slit in the top centre of the barrel, by levering the knife blade gently upwards, releasing pressure as soon as a crack occurs.

4. Slice a scoop from the underside of the pen, to about half its diameter, and centred on the slit.

5. Shape the nib on one side of the slit.

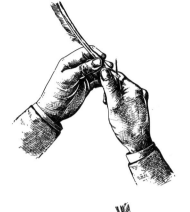

6. Shape the nib on the opposite side, making the two halves match.

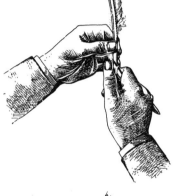

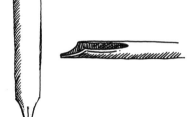

7. If the underside of the nib is too concave, scrape it flat with a clean scoop, removing as little quill as possible.

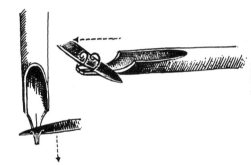

8. To "nib" the pen, rest the underside of the point on a smooth, hard surface. Thin the tip from the top side by pushing the blade forward at a shallow angle; then make a vertical cut, either at right angles to the slit or obliquely. On a very strong feather the last cut can be repeated to remove a very fine sliver, avoiding roughness on the underside of the writing edge.

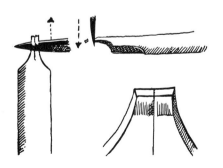

saboc autem   dequinacus

genuit achim   efi ihs quinoa

achim autem   uir ~ xps ·

genuit eliud   Qhieserço

eliud autem   generationes

genuit eleazar   ababracham

eleazar autem   usque adoain

genuit macha   generationes

Above. The *Book of Kells* was never quite completed. This page has only a pale ink outline, and the first colour, yellow, filled in. *Right.* By making detailed tracings of only a small section of the page *opposite*, we can learn more about the work of the Irish artists than any words can tell us.

Letters were carefully spaced and deliberately formed, as we can see in the built-up tops and feet of the letters (serifs). Where the ink has faded, the separate strokes which make up the shapes are revealed. *Opposite*. This rare Coptic textile made around the 6th century suggests that the Irish scribes might have been influenced by designs from the East.

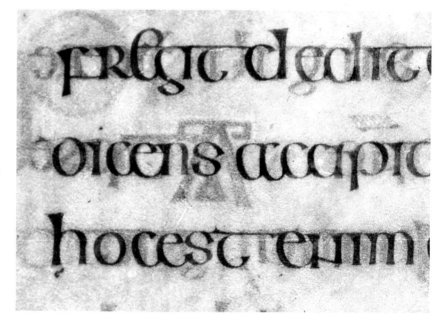

almost inaccessible; and that these remarkable artists had a knowledge and experience of the chemical properties of colours which their successors in the later Middle Ages gladly rejected in favour of more manageable substitutes. The *Book of Kells* is an astonishing tribute to their energy and technical sophistication in those dark times.

The colours were bound together with gelatine glue or by mixing them with a "glair" (egg-white) and water, which prevents the powder from brushing away from the page and gives it depth and a slight sheen. The application of colours and binding materials, too, requires the finest judgement: if there is too little the colours do not fix on the page, but if there is too much the glair or glue will contract when it dries, and pull itself away from the surface. Throughout the work colours are glazed on top of other colours: a solid base colour was applied, and over it a variety of semi-transparent colours were floated to create different shades and depths. The dark brown writing ink was made from gallic acid, a crystalline substance obtained from gall nuts, the nut-like growths produced on oak trees by the gall-wasp's deposit of eggs on the bark. The acid was soaked out of the dried galls with water and mixed with a solution of iron salt which turned the colourless acid into a purplish black, although it later sometimes faded to the brown colour we see in the writing of *Kells*.

It is curious that, despite the minute and lavish care taken over the production of the *Book of Kells*, and the enamel-like jewellery of every page, the text is nonetheless full of mistakes. It is in places carelessly written, containing numerous errors. Parts of sentences are omitted, a whole page is repeated by accident, letters had to be rewritten to replace incorrect ones, and there are other defects in the organisation. Yet the interesting thing is that there are so few attempts to correct the errors. What seemed to matter most to the scribes who made this book was the

magical pictorial imagery they were weaving for the eye of the mind. They even sometimes made fun of their mistakes, drawing attention to them with the pointing hand of a mocking, gawking figure in the margin. The text of some of the most magnificent pages of calligraphy are almost unintelligible, and like many another ambitious artistic project the *Book of Kells* was never quite completed.

By the end of the seventh century the major Roman book scripts, the uncial and half-uncial, had fallen into decay along with the torpor and confusion which followed the break-up of the old world. The process of change from majuscule letters to formal minuscule scripts which had occured in northern Britain was universally echoed by similar developments elsewhere, and a welter of different national minuscule scripts emerged. They included the *Insular* scripts of northern Britain and Ireland; *Anglo-Saxon*; the *Merovingian* script of the Franks; *Visigothic* from Spain; and the *Beneventan* style of the scribes of southern Italy – each of them jostling for superiority, and each considerably influenced by the vigorous fluency of the cursive styles used in the courtroom, accounting-house and civil service, and for vernacular everyday purposes. The Insular script of the *Book of Kells*, for example, may have been based on the Roman half-uncial, but it developed into a national style of great individuality, which survived in Ireland for another seven hundred years. In England the cursive Anglo-Saxon minuscule style also long continued for vernacular use. If Europe had remained as it was in those times, a mass of small warring tribal states without any centralised cultural impulse other than the far-away influence of the Church in Rome, these scripts would have continued to develop in isolation into a myriad of distinct and remote national writing styles. But Europe was now on the brink of just such a unifying impulse, brought about by the dedication, energy and ruthlessness of one man – Charlemagne.

5. The Carolingian Minuscule

Opposite. A French ivory carving, 960–80, showing St Gregory at his desk dictated to by the Holy Spirit, the dove, speaking the divine words into his ear. Humble monastic scribes crouch at his feet writing with quills, and one holding an ink horn.

The Emperor Charlemagne was born on 2 April 742, and died in Aachen on 28 January 814. He was king of the Franks for forty-six years, and by conquest he united almost all the Christian lands of Western Europe, and ruled an empire unrivalled in its unity since the decline of Rome. The conditions which allowed the Franks to emerge as the leading power in Europe had been created some centuries before Charlemagne's birth. The Franks were a non-Christian branch of the West German people, who had in the fourth century settled in part of modern Belgium and along the middle Rhine. They were formidable warriors and first became prominent in Europe when their king, Clovis, in the early sixth century, was baptised to Christianity in the Roman Church in Rheims, and thereby received the support of the Gallo-Roman hierarchy for his defeat of the heretical Burgundians and Visigoths. He became master of Gaul, and founded the Merovingian dynasty which ruled the kingdom of the Franks from 507 to 751.

This support from the Roman Church, which continued almost unabated through one hundred and fifty years of disastrously brutal and chaotic rule by the Merovingians (their government has been described, in a well-known phrase, as "despotism tempered by assassination"), and through the seizure of Church lands on a vast scale by Charles Martel, was finally vindicated by the emergence of Charlemagne himself. He was the grandson of Charles Martel (the victor over the Arabs at Poitiers) and the son of Pepin III ("the Short"), who had founded the Carolingian dynasty when he was consecrated king by the Pope St Boniface in 751. Charlemagne was devoted to the cause of Christianity and Roman civilisation, and determined to revive the arts of learning and culture which were on the point of extinction throughout barbarian Europe. He was also a supremely efficient political realist and an energetic and determined soldier; and this remarkable combination of qualities enabled him to leave an indelible mark on the shape of Europe, on the future relations between the Catholic Church and temporal power, and on European culture and civilisation in general. He began by surrounding himself with learned men, whom he recruited from every corner of the civilised world: from Italy, Paul the Deacon, the historian of the Lombards, and the grammarian Peter of Pisa; from Spain Theodulf the Visigoth; and the greatest of them all, from England, Alcuin of York. Charlemagne reformed the civil and ecclesiastical law, and revived the study of history, grammar and theology, as well as the writings of the poets of antiquity. He founded schools under the aegis of bishoprics and monasteries, in which the highest standards were to be set for the translation and copying of the classical texts.

When the only means of reproducing books was the laborious process

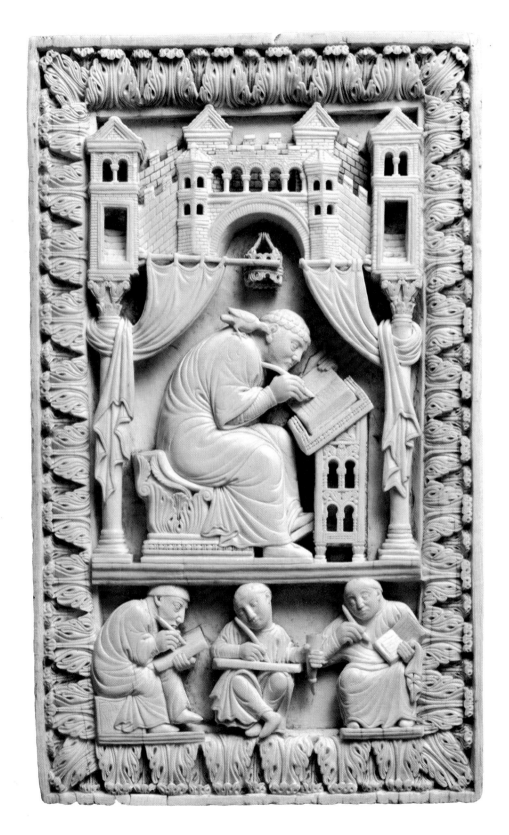

of copying every letter and word by hand, and when the copyists themselves were often deficient in their knowledge of Latin and other languages, it was inevitable that the texts would become corrupted. Errors went undiscovered or – through apathy – uncorrected. In the course of time succeeding copyists would repeat the mistakes in a text, which would eventually become enshrined as authentic. Another factor in this process may well have arisen from the practice whereby past scholars had annotated the margins of the pages. If these notes were not erased later copyists were capable of mistaking them for the text itself and including them within it, to the great confusion of later readers.

Under Charlemagne's instigation, and with intense and Germanic serious-mindedness, the massive task began of putting right the effects of centuries of neglect and confusion in the copying of texts of every kind: the classical works of history, philosophy, grammar and poetry, devotional works, treatises on science, mathematics and law, and the gospels themselves. The new texts were to be derived from the most authentic sources in the libraries of Rome and Monte Cassino, they were to be "correct" and "uniform", they must be "well-edited" and executed "with all possible care". Again and again we find the annotation *ex authentico libro* in the Carolingian manuscripts, signifying that they were authenticated transcriptions made to the highest standard that scholarship and calligraphy could attain.

Alcuin of York, the Anglo-Saxon who had trained with an Irish master, was sent to supervise the school at the Abbey of St Martin at Tours. At this time he was responsible for a recension of the text of the Vulgate (the Latin Bible), and for revising the liturgical books to conform with the traditions of the Roman Church—and this revision is still the basis of the present-day Roman mass book in Latin. Theodulf the Visigoth was sent to Orleans, Angilbert the Frank to Centula and others to Salzburg and Lyons. These great scholars spread their standards and principles throughout Western Christendom, and in countless monasteries scribes would occupy themselves in copying out not only Bibles, gospel books and liturgical calendars, but the works of Virgil and other classical writers. It is to these scholars and scribes that we owe much of our knowledge of the classics.

This "crowd of scribes" (*turba scriptorum*), as Alcuin called it in one of his poems, developed the writing style known as the Carolingian minuscule, with its remarkable clarity and simple beauty, which became readily accepted throughout Charlemagne's dominions. It was the outcome of a fusion of several distinct national styles, all of which themselves had developed out of the classical Roman and informal cursive styles of earlier centuries. The formal texts of the fourth-century Roman church, the Insular writing of Kells and Lindisfarne, and the uncials of Anglo-Saxon Canterbury in the seventh century were still majuscule scripts; that is, they were capital letters written separately. Increasingly in the seventh and eighth centuries different families of pre-Carolingian minuscule (or what in the post-printing age we call "lower-case") scripts had begun to emerge as formal bookhands in the various centres of European learning. In Spain an early medieval best-seller, *The*

The evolution of the Carolingian minuscule. Among the scripts which preceded its development were (from top) Merovingian, Visigothic, Anglo-Saxon, Insular and Beneventan. At the bottom is an early Carolingian script, from the mid-8th century. *Opposite.* The official signature of the Emperor Charlemagne. It has been deduced that the letters forming his name (Karolus) were built up in these stages. Incomplete examples have been found, which suggest that he himself contributed only the two final marks forming the latter A in the diamond-shaped O.

Etymologies by Isidore, Bishop of Seville, which was one of the most widely read books in Europe for two hundred years, may have helped to spread the influence of the Visigothic script to Western Europe; and many Spanish scribes and scholars had left Spain for northern Europe during the Islamic invasions, taking their writing skills with them. Another distinct minuscule script was developed in southern Italy, known as the Beneventan style, which although not adopted widely outside the area of its source, Monte Cassino, enjoyed a long life and was still being used as late as the thirteenth century in Italy.

Close ties between the Anglo-Saxons of Britain and the Saxons and Franks of their continental homelands ensured that the minuscule scripts of southern Britain were well travelled among the German peoples with whom the priest St Boniface, for instance, spent twenty years working as a missionary at the beginning of the eighth century. The evangelising zeal of the Irish monks during the years leading up to the accession of Charlemagne took their Insular version of the minuscule script to the monasteries of Europe too, and the eventual distribution of all the pre-tenth-century manuscripts of both the Anglo-Saxon and Insular styles which are known still to exist tell their own story of the way in which the scripts could travel and possibly influence other peoples at that time. Of some 425 manuscripts including charters, only just over 100 remain in the islands of Britain, and the rest are still in the libraries of Europe: between 40 and 50 in Switzerland; 4 in France; 40 to 50 in the Vatican library in Rome; and 150 in Germany of which the largest single collection, over 30 manuscripts, still remains in the library at Würzburg.

Finally, nearer "home", under the Merovingian kings Frankish scribes had produced a cursive minuscule which, as E. A. Lowe puts it, "may well have formed the strongest of all the roots from which the Carolingian minuscule derived its ultimate form".

The Carolingian classical revival also renewed interest in the inscriptional lettering of Roman times, and a hierarchical order of scripts was developed: the great square- and half-square-based Roman inscriptional capitals were reinstated at the head, the full rounded uncial script for chapter headings; and even the rustic style of capital or majuscule would be incorporated in the design in descending order of rank. Finally, the Carolingian minuscule itself brought an air of calm and spaciousness to the whole body of the text. The regularity and order of this approach to calligraphic design was reflected also in the organisation of the schools in which it was practised, and even in such details as the prescribed rules for the writing of each letter, and the angle at which the pen should be held. We have a first-hand account of the sound of scribes at work in the scriptorium: it was like the humming of bees as the copying scribes mumbled to themselves the words of the texts lying in front of them.

For everyday writing at this time the wax tablet and stylus which the Greeks and Romans used was still commonly employed. Vellum was too expensive for ephemeral use. Indeed even in the scriptoria it was so precious that older texts were frequently scraped away and re-used for the writing of modern ones. It is tragic to think of the literary and artistic

The Grandval Bible, a Carolingian manuscript written at Tours around 840. The details of the initial H have more in common with the wall paintings of Pompeii and Herculaneum than with the Celtic extravagances of the jeweller's craft. The hierarchical arrangement of scripts, the use of capitals descending to small letters, was refined during this period.

INCIPIT LIBER
EXODVS

AECSVNT (
NOMINA
FILIORŪ
ISRAHEL
QVIINGRES
SISVNTIN
AEGYPTŪ
CVMIACOB
SINGVLI
CVMDOMI
BVSSVIS
INTROIE
RVNT

Ruben. symeon. leui. luda. issachar. zabulon
etbeniamin. danetnepthalim. gad etaser
Erantigitur omnes animae eorum quaeegres
sae sunt defemore iacob. septuaginta quinque
Joseph autem. inaegypto erat Quomortuo et
uniuersis fratrib: eius omniq. cognatione sua.
filii isrt creuerunt. et quasi germinantes multi
plicati sunt acroborati nimis impleuer terra

Making notes with a stylus on a wax-coated diptych (from a 12th-century manuscript made at Bamberg).

Scraping sheepskin with a half-moon knife.

Cutting out the sheet.

Sharpening a pen.

treasures that must have been destroyed in this way. Papyrus was still used in Rome by the papal scribes for some important documents (rather than books), and would be until well into the eleventh century. It was usually sold in rolls of twenty or fifty sheets glued together, with the horizontal fibres on the inside.

Despite the success of the Carolingian minuscule in colonising the writing practices of all Europe, enclaves of resistance remained, and the most important of these was the Roman curia itself, the seat of papal authority and the centre of Christendom. The officials of the curia did not use a script which everyone could read. They used instead the *littera Romana*, what E. A. Lowe describes as "Rome's unique medieval contribution to handwriting," a fearfully arcane and difficult script which must have strained the eyes and puzzled the minds of many a bishop and king throughout Christian Europe. As Lowe says, "Art does not flourish in an atmosphere of bureaucracy".

The missionary zeal of the Church in Eastern Europe was confronted by a new problem. The Slavic peoples had no alphabets, and their languages were ill-suited to the unaltered adaptation of the Roman or Greek scripts. The Croats (in 700) and the Poles (in 999) were converted to Roman Catholicism, and religious texts were provided for them in an alphabet derived from the Latin, and modified to meet the phonetic demands of their languages. The Serbs, Bulgars and Russians, on the other hand, were converted to "Orthodox" Christianity under the authority of the Eastern Empire of Constantinople; and likewise a new alphabet was needed for the transliteration of their languages. Two versions of such an alphabet were produced, known as the Glagolitic and the Cyrillic, variously attributed to the missionary and diplomatist St Cyril and to his brother Methodius in the mid-ninth century, under the authority of the Emperor Michael III. It is ironic that the Cyrillic alphabet, which first brought the Christian gospels to the Russian people in the ninth century, is now associated with the colonising zeal of another great orthodoxy in the twentieth.

After Charlemagne's death work carried on in the scriptoria of the palace school and in the monasteries. In Rheims the artists employed by Bishop Ebo produced illuminations in a highly individual style in the classical mode; and in Tours (until 850 when it was plundered by the Normans) some of the greatest works of Carolingian manuscript art were produced in the years following the death of the Emperor. Charlemagne's successors, the Emperor Lothar I (843–55) and Charles the Bald (843–77), King of the Western Franks, continued to commission manuscripts for their pleasure and edification and to distribute as diplomatic gifts, and the productions of their scriptoria were thus diffused throughout the Western world. Magnificent books were produced, many of which survive, and they remain as proof of the wide-ranging and international vision of Charlemagne. The techniques which the illuminators displayed in their handling of gold and silver decoration owe much to the technology of Islam and Byzantium, where gilding with the use of gum and thinly beaten gold-leaf was highly developed. The design of the scripts represents the triumphant fusion of diverse antique as well as eighth-century national styles, and the artists who decorated the pages of the Carolingian books also display a mastery over the virile decorative designs of Celtic interlace, the writhing animal forms of Anglo-Saxon jewellery and the sophisticated painting of modelled human form and drapery as fine as any that have been found from late antiquity.

Scraping out a mistake.

In the story of Western writing there are only two major landmarks upon which all later developments depend: the first is the final realisation of the alphabetic system itself – based on phonetic principles – achieved by the ancient Greeks and modified by the Romans. The second is the "invention" of the minuscule family of formal scripts, of which the Carolingian strain represents a standard of simplicity and beauty against which all other writing styles can be measured, and which despite the later experiments of the Gothic period continues to serve us as well as it did the court of Charlemagne twelve hundred years ago.

Although in the tenth century the stability of the emerging kingdoms of Europe was far from established, one thing that was sure and strong was the growing power of the Christian Church. There was now an increasing optimism and energy in European culture, as the people recovered from the debilitating centuries of Viking, Saracen and Hungarian raids. Churches were built everywhere in an immensely wide variety of styles. Everywhere, but particularly in France, the excitement of experiment and the spirit of enquiry were being re-born. At the same time an astonishing growth took place in the spread and influence of monasticism. Thousands of new monasteries were founded, and the structure and form of monastic life became the subject of numerous, repeated and thorough-going reforms. The monastic tradition was of course far from new, and indeed most of the reforming principles originating in the tenth and eleventh centuries were no more than a return, in one aspect or another, to the Rule which St Benedict had instituted in the sixth century. But there was a difference, deriving largely from the events in Europe during the preceding 500 years: the monk was no longer in retreat from the chaos and devastation of the world, but was now regarded as a member of a spiritual elite, a soldier of Christ.

Sewing the gatherings of pages.

St Benedict's Rule provided that certain hours of the day should be set aside for manual labour, and craftsmen should be allowed to practise their craft. But they were not to allow their skill to be a source of temptation to pride, and any monk found guilty of boasting was to be removed from his work until he had suitably humbled himself. The artist, therefore, was encouraged not to develop his gifts as an expression of his own individuality but to put them to the service of God. Many books were made during the centuries of monastic book-production which indeed capture the sense that they were created as an act of piety and worship. No doubt most of these books were the product of teamwork, but from time to time their monkish creators specifically claim sole responsibility for the writing and illumination. It must always have been tempting to break away from one's brotherly or sisterly anonymity and insert a small personal signature out of pride or for posterity's sake. Eadwine,

Shaping up the wooden boards for the cover with an axe.

Fixing clasps or bindings.

the scribe of Christchurch, Canterbury, who is portrayed in a manuscript of about 1140, evidently had no such scruples. Around his portrait he proclaimed himself to be the prince of writers: "Neither my fame nor my praise will die quickly; demand of my letters who I am. . . . Fame proclaims you in your writing for ever Eadwine, you are to be seen here in the painting. The worthiness of this book demonstrates your excellence. O God, this book is given to You by him. Receive this acceptable gift." We hope God was grateful!

It is only fair to add that Eadwine's trumpet-blast of self-congratulation was partly concealed in the form of a riddle, a common form of monastic diversion. In the eighth century the Abbot of Jarrow, for example, inscribed a riddle about his quill pen:

> *In kind simple am I, nor gain from anywhere wisdom,*
> *But now each man of wisdom always traces my footsteps.*
> *Habiting now broad earth, high heav'n I formerly wandered.*
> *Though I am seen to be white, I leave black traces behind me.*

There are countless imprecations to be found written by scribes against the careless handling of manuscripts. Even the humble bookworm was attacked in a disdainful little riddle:

> *I thrive on letters, yet no letters know,*
> *I live in books, not made more studious so,*
> *Devour the muses, but no wiser grow.*

The work of a monkish scribe was long and arduous, broken only by prayer and Holy Days, and every daylight hour was a working one. Yet one ninth-century Irish scribe found time to write a tranquil note in the margin of a book he was writing or studying, translated as: "Pleasant to me is the glittering of the sun today upon these margins, because it flickers so."

Some scribes still worked from dictation, as we can see from the blatant spelling mistakes, added letters and duplicated syllables which could never have occurred if they were copying direct from an exemplar; and sometimes these errors give us an intriguing insight into the way Latin or Greek was pronounced at the time and place they were written. They also help us judge how many scribes might have been employed on an individual book, since some sections are distinctly better spelt than others.

Nuns and monks sometimes worked together in the copying and illuminating of texts, whether in separate communities or in the many double monasteries which had been founded in Europe since the idea was first introduced in Egypt in the sixth century. In an astronomical treatise made in Alsace about 1154, Brother Sintram the illuminator has left us a record of such teamwork by painting on the dedication page a portrait of himself and of Guta the scribe: she was a canoness of the sister house in nearby Schwartzenthann. Women in holy orders continued to produce books and to collaborate with monks in doing so until the later Middle Ages.

Alongside these glorious achievements in the art of formal writing and

Right. Eadwine, monk of Canterbury, the self-proclaimed "prince of writers" (*c.* 1140). *Below.* A female scribe: Adelhard the nun, who signed her work and added this small self-portrait.

illumination, everyday scribble continued in just the same way as it does today. As we have seen, the wax tablet and stylus were still used for the purpose. The tablets of wood coated with coloured wax were often folded into a leather-hinged booklet or small diptych which could be worn on the belt. In the year 1200 St Hugh dreamed that a great pear tree in his garden at Lincoln had fallen to the ground, and what worried him most was the waste of its timber, "for so many diptyches could be cut from it that there would be more than enough for the scholastic studies of the whole of England and France".

Another riddle was inspired by these everyday tools of the scribe:

St Bernard.

> *Of honey-laden bees I first was born,*
> *But in the forest grew my outer coat;*
> *My tough backs come from shoes. An iron point*
> *In artful wanderings cuts a fair design,*
> *And leaves long, twisted furrows, like a plough . . .*

Orderic Vitalis at the end of the eleventh century tells us how he had been shown a book by Anthony, a monk of Winchester, which he was most anxious to copy, "but in truth, since the bearer was in haste to depart and the winter cold prevented me from writing, I made a full and accurate abbreviation on tablets [of wax], and now I shall endeavour to entrust it, summarily, to parchment". Complaints about stiff and frozen hands were a common theme in the marginal jottings of the monastic scribes, and this was not the first mention of a monk putting off the writing of the final script until warmer weather came along.

The sumptuous productions of the Benedictine scriptoria were not always received with unqualified enthusiasm by other orders. St Jerome, in the late fourth century, had already roundly condemned the waste and luxury of "those who have ancient books written in gold and silver on purple parchment"; and St Bernard, who joined the community at Cîteaux in 1112 and made the Cistercian order famous, waged continual war on what he regarded as the self-indulgent waste of the carved stones, silk albs and gold plate of Cluny and other monasteries. "What think you the purpose of all this? Those monstrous centaurs, those half-men? . . . So many and so marvellous are the varieties of shapes on every hand that we are more tempted to read in the marble than in books . . . . For God's sake, if men are not ashamed of these follies, why at least do they not shrink from the expense?" A statute in the Cistercian rule ordained that manuscripts were to be written in ink of one colour, and without illumination.

By the end of the twelfth century, however, the Church's monopoly of scholarship and learning began gradually to decline, and the monastic scriptoria ceased to be the main centres of book production. Long before this professional lay scribes had been admitted into the monasteries to work alongside the monks. Increasingly, the power of the Church was tempered by the spreading influence of the emerging merchant class. In the towns where the prosperous merchants built their tall houses huddled within the shadow of the giant cathedral churches of the land-rich bishops, professional scribes set up their workshops, formed themselves into guilds and wrote out legal documents and jewelled books for princes, merchants and lawyers, prayer books for their ladies, and educational texts for their student sons.

This secularisation of society led to the founding of universities and schools that had no direct link with the Church. In Italy the law school at Bologna and the school of medicine at Salerno were among the first of such secular institutions. The first great university was born in France, where in the late twelfth century a cathedral school at Paris had so far established its reputation throughout Europe that it was granted separate legal recognition and became the most important of all centres for the study of theology and arts. The foundation of universities at Oxford, Naples, Padua and many other cities in Europe followed in the next half century, often under the patronage of emperors and kings.

To these institutions students from many countries came to prepare themselves for a career in the Church or at court, and to learn from the great theologians who taught in them. Since Latin was still the *lingua franca* throughout all Europe a student could choose to study at Seville or Bologna just as well as at Paris or Oxford.

The influence of Islam in European culture played a considerable part in this process of the secularisation of scholarship. From the tenth century pilgrimages to the Holy Places of Jerusalem had been possible, and links had been restored between that city and the scholastic centres of Europe. The Norman reconquest of Sicily and southern Italy opened new links with Islamic culture and technology, as did the presence of Moorish Spain on the southern fringe of Europe. In 1085 Alphonso VI of Spain proclaimed himself emperor in both the Islamic and Christian rites, and the see of Toledo grew into a centre of learning in science and medicine based on Arab models which were far more advanced than anything yet achieved in Europe.

The texts of Aristotle and Euclid did not come to us direct from the cities of Athens or Alexandria; many of them were first reintroduced to the West by translations made by the Islamic scholars of Toledo. The philosophy, science and mythology of Greece had been transcribed in Arabic by Islamic scholars when the Arabs occupied the Greek colonies in Egypt in 642, and it was through their custodianship of classical Greek culture that it was first transmitted westwards to the medieval universities and cathedral schools of Europe. One man, Gerard of Cremona, who died in Toledo in 1187, reputedly translated no fewer than seventy-one Arab works on astronomy, astrology and mathematics, as well as medical and philosophical works.

The Arabs brought not only the old scholarship, but new technology. As early as the mid-eighth century Arab traders had acquired the Chinese techniques of making paper from rags; although several hundred years were still to pass before the "cloth parchment" of Moorish Spain found its great vocation in the West as a vital ingredient in the spread of the invention of a certain Herr Gutenberg and his followers, the "ditto device" which was to turn the world of learning on its head.

Arabic numerals

AD 976

Late 12th century

Late 14th century

6. The Middle Ages

Right. The artist in his workshop visited by a noble patron, the tools of his trade scattered on the table before him. *Opposite.* A French example of the kind of sumptuous books made for the rich by the workshops in the towns and cities.

The labour of the writer is the refreshment of the reader. The one depletes the body, the other advances the mind. Whoever you are, therefore, do not scorn but rather be mindful of the work of the one labouring to bring you profit . . . If you do not know how to write you will consider it no hardship, but if you want a detailed account of it let me tell you that the work is heavy: it makes the eyes misty, bows the back, crushes the ribs and belly, brings pain to the kidneys, and makes the body ache all over. Therefore, O reader, turn the leaves gently and keep your fingers away from the letters, for as the hailstorm ruins the harvest of the land so does the unserviceable reader destroy the book and the writing. As the sailor finds welcome the final harbour, so does the scribe the final line. Deo gratias semper.

Colophon from *Silos Beatus*, twelfth century

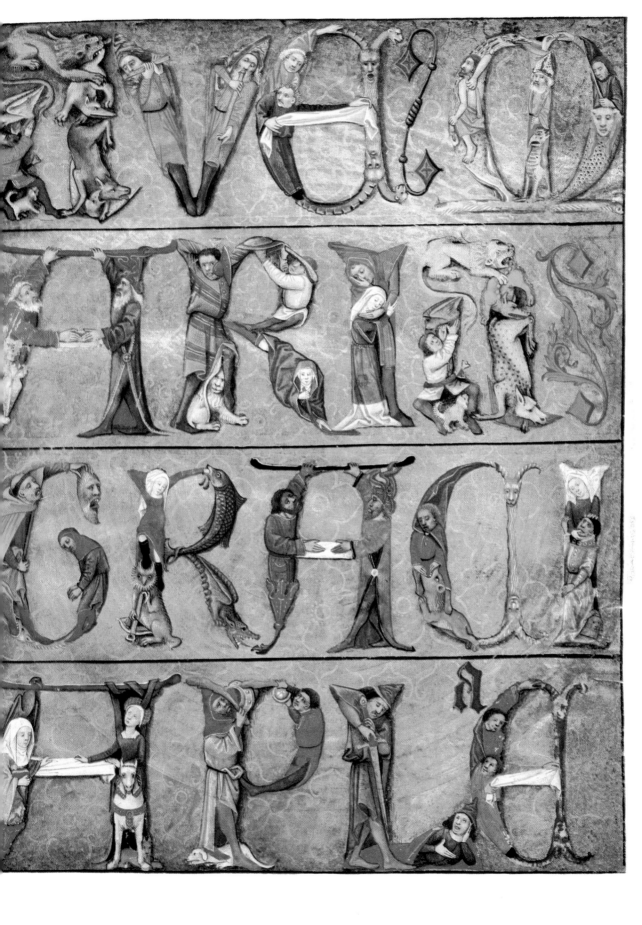

Charlemagne's empire and the dynasty he founded had ended by the end of the tenth century; but the heritage of the Carolingian minuscule continued to be transmitted to each generation of scribes for four more centuries. As time passed, however, small variations and alterations were made, so that the compressed and angular Gothic script which emerged by the thirteenth century bore little resemblance to its forbear. Apart from practical considerations, which have always influenced the shape of writing styles, there were also the discernible influences of fashion and style which had changed rapidly over the same period, and which can be seen in many of the arts and artifacts of the time. The rounded, arched letters of the school of Charlemagne are echoed in the windows and doorways of his palace-chapel at Aachen, while the pointed angularity of the northern Gothic script is everywhere seen in the architecture of its time. Furthermore, the Gothic of the north with its densely packed lines of stark black shapes was quite different from its counterpart in the warmer south. The pointed style never took a firm hold in Italy, for example, where a more open version of it called Rotunda or Italian Gothic was developed. Wherever the scribes lived and worked they no doubt unconsciously absorbed and transmuted the influence of their time, and they expressed them in the shapes of the letters they wrote.

Until the 12th century the production of books had been primarily aimed at two markets: luxurious books for the courts of kings and princes, and theological works and service books for the Church. But as Arab, Greek and Jewish scholarship led the way to the creation of independent centres of learning a need appeared for a wider range of books, for the works of Aristotle and other ancient philosophers, and treatises on logic, mathematics, music and astronomy. For the first time a vernacular literature began to appear: writers like Dante and Chaucer wrote in their native languages, and were able to direct their work to a wider and at the same time more local audience, the emerging mercantile classes centred around the towns and cities of Europe. These needs were met by the appearance of flourishing lay workshops of craftsmen, scribes, bookbinders, illuminators and parchmenters. A prosperous merchant could now ape the practice of kings and commission handwritten books decorated for his pleasure and instruction. He might order books on hunting, agriculture, food and health, astrology, and household manuals, as well as romances and the works of popular authors such as Christine de Pisan, the tales of Roland and elaborately decorated books on courtly love.

The scribes and illuminators who formed this new class of professional craftsmen have left us some evidence of the life they led and the kind of people they were, much of it to be found in or deduced from the work they produced. We hear of Egbert the left-handed scribe, John the one-eyed scribe, the scribe who added small footnotes such as "let the scribe have a goose for his pains", and the husband and wife team who left their signature "Alan the scribe and his wife the illuminator". Often working in groups or teams, these craftsmen took commissions on a fixed price and with a set deadline. Through their efforts the output of

Neither the artist nor his assistant portrayed in this initial from a manuscript produced at a religious house around 1150 are monks. While the artist paints the letter S his assistant grinds colour on a stone slab with a muller.

books in Europe increased enormously at this time, but even so they barely kept up with the growing demands of a new public. Richard de Bury, Bishop of Durham in the mid-fourteenth century, may not perhaps have been typical in being obsessed with collecting books: he is reported to have had more than fifteen hundred handwritten books in his personal library, "enough to fill five carts".

The craft workshops in cities like Oxford, Paris and Bologna were often grouped together in close-knit communities, much as small trades still are in the cities of Europe and America. A workshop would tend to specialise in one part of the production of books, and by the 1350s the principal divisions of the trade had become established. The writers of the main body of the book, and the limners who illuminated the pages, gathered themselves into separate and increasingly powerful guilds or fraternities to control and protect their valued "mysteries" against "unfair" competition. The guild of text writers in the city of York even as late as 1495 felt it necessary to force through an ordinance which prevented priests (who may well have been subsidised by their communities) from copying out documents for profit if their salaries from other sources exceeded eight marks per year. In Hereford the stationers and booksellers shared a guild with the haberdashers, barbers and painters. The text writers of York were joined by the limners, the turnours who drew initial letters and borders, the notours who were responsible for musical notation, and the flourishers. These were often family businesses, in which sons would tend to follow their fathers; and daughters and wives are known to have taken over their father's or husband's workshops or worked alongside them in the production of books.

During the last year of his apprenticeship in the workshop of a master craftsman, a young man would devote some of his time to preparing an example of his best work to present to the master and wardens of his guild. If this so-called "masterpiece" was of the required standard, he would qualify as a journeyman scribe, which implied that before he settled down to employ others he was expected to work away from the immediate vicinity of his master's shop.

A customer might choose the style, standard or price he wanted by going from the workshop of one specialist to another, or more probably he went to the "stationer", a bookseller who stayed in one place and performed the function of a middle-man, co-ordinating the work of the different craftsmen and, when times were slack, commissioning new books to sell ready-made in the shop. While the master craftsman and his apprentices who worked in the town would be paid in cash, the journeyman would often be paid at least partly in kind. In the 1320s the Countess of Clare employed a scribe at Clare Castle for sixteen weeks to write a book. His payment was eight shillings, plus board and lodging. The book contains some three hundred and seventeen thousand words, so if he worked six days a week including Holy Days he produced three thousand, three hundred words a day (and was paid less than a penny a day).

Throughout Europe, contracts were often drawn up for the production of books, specifying the financial arrangements and often including

Medieval monks continued to produce books, but often in close cooperation with outside lay craftsmen. These initials made in mid-13th-century Germany show scenes in the process of making a book. Clockwise from the top, the parchmenter shows a finished skin to a monk; the scribe rules out lines for the text; a lay artist paints a portrait, steadying his right hand with his left; and sheets of vellum are trimmed to size.

penalty clauses to ensure that the work was finished on time. An indenture or contract between Robert Brekeling "scriptor" and John Forbor for the Dean and Chapter of York Minster in 1346 provides for Robert to write a psalter with a calendar, for a set sum of money, and in the same size writing to complete the office for the dead, hymns and collect. He was also to illuminate the first letters of the psalms in gold and colour. The indenture specifies that the first letters of the verses of the psalms should be in "good" blue and vermilion, that all letters at the beginning of the nocturns should be five lines high, except for the beginning of the psalter where the *Beatus Vir* and *Dixit Dominus* had to be six or seven lines high. For this work he received an allowance in addition to his pay of 1s 6d for gold and 2s for colour; and he was to be given one robe, a blanket, a sheet and a pillow.

By the late 12th century the rounded Carolingian script had become so compressed that almost all the curves were excluded. These examples are from the 10th, 12th and 14th centuries. *Opposite and Below.* O is the mother of the alphabet. As it became compressed so did all the other letters based on it.

A scribe was expected to master the different styles and hands appropriate to different kinds of text, and it may well have been the pressures of the new commercialism which brought about the first great change in style since the development of the Carolingian minuscule in the ninth century. Towards the end of the twelfth century the round, fat shapes of the Carolingian letter were squeezed thinner and thinner until almost all the curves were excluded, and the compressed and upright Gothic letter emerged. This style allowed far more words to be crammed onto the page, particularly if the text was arranged in a two-column layout: and it has been calculated that a book in this style needed as little as one third of the page area required by open Carolingian letters of the same height. The medieval term for this upright and closely-packed book hand was Textus (from the Latin *texere*, to weave). The scriveners or writers of the court letter widely adopted the more rapid cursive version of it for legal documents, faint vestiges of which still occur in the "Whereas's" of modern legal deeds.

The scribe's apprentice would start off with the humbler workshop tasks such as ruling lines, grinding and mulling the colours on a stone slab and mixing them with a variety of traditional media such as yolk and white of egg. For most of the crafts an apprenticeship of at least seven years was required. Although most of the manual skills and tricks of the trade could be learned in a shorter time by a competent young person, it was evidently felt that the maturing of vision and attitudes of mind which have to be brought to bear on the production of finely-wrought pieces were an essential element in the education of the artist-craftsman.

Very few examples have survived of what seem to be genuine attempts to produce a treatise or workshop instruction book for professional scribes and illuminators. Even Cennino Cennini's famous work *Il Libro dell' Arte*, which gives students a great deal of sound general advice, is, in parts, curiously unsatisfactory. He urges the student to submit himself to the direction of a master for instruction as early as possible, and not to leave until he has to; to eat and drink moderately; and to preserve the steadiness of his hand by avoiding such heavy work as heaving stones with a crowbar and indulging too much in the company of women. Yet when he instructs us to use a town hen's egg to paint the flesh colours of a young person, but a farm-egg yolk for the aged and swarthy, one has the uncomfortable suspicion that these are the words of an interviewing journalist rather than a practising artisan. In many such works too much is left unsaid to be of practical, as opposed to general or literary, interest. It has been assumed that this tendency in the medieval compendia was the result of the author taking certain processes, the knowledge of which has since been lost, for granted in his readers' experience. Two anonymous eleventh- and twelfth-century manuscripts have survived, *Compendium artis picturae* and *De Clarea*, which ring so true, however, that the work of other compilers seems like hearsay in comparison.

Both of these rare manuscripts, oddly enough, deal with the same problem: the technical management of colour, which is one of the hardest things to teach a beginner. Many of the basic colours of the scribe are made from dry pigments mixed with water and held together with a medium. If the binding is too thin the colour when it dries will simply return to powder and rub away from the surface. If the binding mixture is too strong – whether of glair or fish glue – it will contract when it dries, the colour will crack and it will pull itself away from the surface. It must also flow well off the pen or brush. The *Compendium artis picturae* talks of adding drops of water to the colour to ensure it stays sufficiently moist before use; and the difficulty of working on skins which are over-dry or hard, or in an atmosphere which is too dry. These are just the kind of words one would expect to hear from a craftsman

Looking at Illuminated Manuscripts

By examining illuminated manuscripts in a methodical way, we can learn a great deal about the techniques used to create them. Look in turn for the following features.

The writing surface may be paper, or skin which has a more velvety nap. Vellum (calfskin) and parchment (sheepskin) are almost impossible to tell apart. With both, the hair side tends to be more cream-coloured than the whiter flesh side, and the remnants of the hair follicles can sometimes be seen as small dots (for example in A, right).

Ruling of lines. The initial prick marks can usually be detected quite easily (B), but several methods were used for ruling lines: for example, scoring with a hard point (A), which made it unnecessary to rule the other side of the sheet; and drawing with a lead plummet or pencil (B, and other examples on this page) or pen and faint ink (C).

Design and texture of the page. The density of the design and appearance of the whole page is controlled by the shaping of individual letters, and by the use of finishing touches to the heads and feet (compare A, C, D and F). Faded ink often reveals the separate strokes used to build up the letters (C). Sometimes we can see, when the writing changes in weight or sharpness, where the scribe re-cut his quill or took up another.

Mistakes were surprisingly common, and may be found crossed out, or scraped away with a knife leaving a rougher surface in which dirt may have collected (C).

Annotations. Distinguish annotations that have been added by later readers (D)

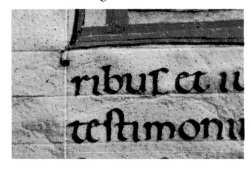

A

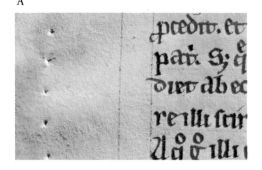

B

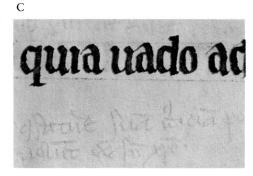

C

D

E

F

G

H

I

J

K

L

M

N

from those inserted at the time. The scribe responsible for the main text in black often left spaces for rubrication and illuminated initials, with lightly written instructions to the illuminator (E). These can be hard to spot: in F the scribe's small r can be seen on the upper right-hand side of the sketched capital.

Colours. Red lead or vermilion, and blue azurite or lapis lazuli inks, require different handling techniques, and a longer slit in the quill (compare A, E, G and I). Red often has a glossy sheen (G), imparted by the egg yolk or white mixed with it.

Illuminated letters. The illuminator's techniques can be detected and reconstructed (see pages 90–91). The stages usually include: first, a pencil sketch, inked in (F) – although this was sometimes ignored (J); then gilding; then the insertion of layers of colour, outlined with black (compare G and H); and finally the white highlights (H and K). Observant readers will have noticed that F, G and H are from the same manuscript, an unfinished 14th-century pontifical.

Gilding. Three kinds of gilding are generally seen: gold leaf on a film of gum (G); gold leaf on a plaster-based gesso, highly burnished (at the foot of L); or powdered gold bound with gum and water, used like paint (on the inner background of K).

Figures were painted and drawn in much the same order as that used for illuminated letters and decorations: a pencil sketch, inked in (N); the build-up of gold, if any, and colours (M); and finally the black outlines and white highlights (L).

used to working with skins. Humidity is still a key factor in the comfortable handling of writing skins, and in the satisfactory use of liquid inks, paints and gilding media. The dry atmosphere of southern California would have been an agony to the medieval scribe, fighting to hold down the hard, undulating vellum with his knife and racing with the evaporation of the ink from the pot with his pen. "Take the greatest possible care not to work in too warm [dry] a place, and to keep your work in a moist atmosphere. If you wish to work on an over-hard, dry parchment, a particularly common fault in goatskins, you will have to leave it for a while in a moist place." There speaks a man who really understood the problems of the working scribe.

The apprentice would have to learn to deal with these problems, as well as the handling of his tools. His work would begin when the sheets of parchment or vellum were delivered from the stationer who had ordered the book, or direct from the parchmenter. He would begin by checking the skin for holes and stains, scraping it with a knife or rubbing it with pumice-stone to raise a slight nap on the surface. This would give a pleasing appearance to the skin, and also help retain the ink and prevent it from spreading as it might on a smoother surface. The hair side of the skin is always easier to work; the fibres are more tightly knit so that it is more tolerant of the knife scraping it smooth. The underside of the skin, the flesh side, is generally a lighter colour and is smoother to begin with; but the fibres are more loosely knit and the slightest over-exertion with pumice or knife would raise the nap to an unacceptably furry and unsightly roughness. It is interesting that this characteristic was put to practical use by the administrators of the English medieval exchequer rolls, who particularly specified the use of the flesh side of cheap parchment precisely because they could quickly discover any erasures or alterations in the accounts.

The next stage was to rule the sheets. Taking a few at a time, with the cream-coloured hair side and the whiter flesh side alternately upwards, they would be folded and pricked through with an awl or a knife point to indicate the margin and to show where the lines were to be ruled. This process ensured that each page in a gathering would match its neighbour perfectly, in the colour of the writing surface, the text area and the line spacing. As we saw in the *Book of Kells*, the earlier practice was to rule the lines with a pointed metal or bone stylus pressed hard along the edge of a ruler, producing a scored line on the hair side of the sheet and a corresponding raised line on the other. After the twelfth century the practice of using a lead pencil or plummet became more common. This would have been a piece of lead set into a handle, or perhaps cut into a disc shape like a tailor's chalk today.

When the skin was ready for writing and the lines were ruled, the scribe would sit at his desk and sharpen his pen, commonly a goose quill. This would often be taken from the first flight feathers of the left wing – the left wing feather curves comfortably around the knuckle of a right-handed person's hand – although any comfortable-sized feather would do. The quill would first be dried or hardened, before being slit and shaped to the width required by the style of script to be copied. The

The apprentice Everwinus sits practising arabesques with a brush, while his master Hildebert has stopped work to throw a sponge at a mouse.

scribe's pen-knife was a personal treasure jealously cared for, specially ground to enable him to make the curved scoops out of the tube-like shape of the quill. The ink would be either carbon-based, or one of the oak-gall mixtures, whichever happened to be more favoured by the master of the workshop.

Transferring his knife to his left hand, the scribe would dip his pen into the inkhorn; and holding down the bumpy vellum sheet with the knife in his left hand he would begin to write. The text he was copying would be within easy sight, and he would be careful to gauge his writing to match the length of line of the copy in front of him, and to leave appropriate spaces for the larger letters which begin each chapter, so that his colleague the illuminator could add his larger decorative letter-ing later. As he completed each page he would take a fine pen and pale ink, and quickly scribble in each blank space the necessary instructions to the illuminator. If the book was to contain rubrics – small initials or headings in red, used to indicate important subjects or sections in the text – the scribe would also write in small pale letters the missing text along the extreme edge of the page, taking care to leave the right space for the missing words, and giving the rubricator the instructions he would later need when filling them in in red. In medieval calendars the saints' days were invariably rubricated: hence our expression "red letter day".

The scribe, of course, would sometimes make mistakes, and in a well-regulated workshop or monastic scriptorium a corrector would be employed to check the work of the scribes. In some cathedrals an official would be specifically delegated the task of ensuring that the books in their charge were corrected, and at Salisbury, for example, the income from a portion of land was annually assigned to pay for the correction of books. The errors that occurred were very much of the kind we ourselves would make when typing or writing a copy: missing words, missing out a line because we look up at the wrong place in the original, repeating a word or a phrase which may have come at the end of a line, and so on. Sometimes the scribe himself would spot the mistake. The correction could be made by taking a knife with a moon-shaped blade, or the pen-knife itself, and carefully scraping away the ink from the upper surface of the skin. Vellum is quite tolerant of this, since it is composed of several epidermal layers, particularly compact on the hair side. If the scraping was neatly done, and the skin burnished down, the erasure would be hard to spot at the time; but since it would remain slightly rougher than elsewhere on the page the centuries of dirt that have gathered since disclose the slip to our eyes.

A rare but fascinating example of a different kind of scribal cosmetics has been found on at least two elaborately illuminated "prestige" manu-script books of the fourteenth century. One of them, after a clumsy erasure had failed to eradicate the dark ink which had sunk deep into the surface of the skin, has white paint matching the colour of the vellum stippled over it to disguise the slip. The second book used the same method, but apparently more out of vanity than contrition, because although there was no actual error, white paint was used to lessen the effect of the dark colour used as a base for gilding, which showed through the semi-transparent skin from the other side of the page. Contemporary decoration was added *on top* of the white, and it was so successfully carried out that it has gone unnoticed by generations of scholars who have thumbed its sumptuous pages.

If the corrector found a mistake in the text he would put a neat pencil note in the margin to indicate what the mistake was, and what should go in its place. Sometimes the error was so gross that the only course was to make a clean breast of it. One scribe, having missed out a whole section of the text, had no option but to write out the missing lines in the margin at the bottom of the page, and make fun of his own mistake by having the illuminator crate up the omitted words in a decorative box, harness it with ropes and paint in a team of little men to haul the words contained in the crate to their rightful place in the text. More frequently a missing word which could not be squeezed in was written in the margin in ink, and a helpful pointing finger would show the reader where to place it.

When he reached the end of a gathering of eight or so pages, the scribe would make a mark at the foot of the last page to assist the binder in matching it to the succeeding one – an especially important point when several scribes were working simultaneously on different parts of the same book. A trained scribe working with a limited repertoire of scripts would not have found it difficult to imitate his neighbour very closely— the eye is very forgiving especially of handwritten, as opposed to printed, text. This method was commonly used by the stationer who co-ordinated the work, and he would frequently share out a single book among several ateliers; the scribes and illuminators were supplied exemplars in pieces, sometimes with instructions appropriate to the customer's individual wishes.

A damaged manuscript shows exactly how it was sometimes done; the paint has fallen off the illumination, and under it the instructions are revealed, written in a small and hasty script: "Make the tomb by which Saul and his servant stand, and two men, jumping over a ditch, who talk to him and announce that the asses have been found." Another reads: "Make prophets, one with a cithara, another with a flute, the third one with a drum, and Saul prophesying and his servant with his harp." It only needs the words "by next Friday" for the production-line image to be complete.

Apart from painting interiors of buildings, statues and heraldic work the decoration of books was the most important outlet for the talents of medieval painters. In a mid-twelfth-century survey at Winchester, four painters, one scribe and one parchmenter are listed. The latter two, significantly, were neighbours in Busket Lane, three of the four painters lived in the High Street, and the fourth in Tower Street. Just over a hundred years later, of only two painters listed one was a woman, Agnes, "la paintresse", who held land in Staple Gardens at a rent of four pence. Oxford at this time supported many more: 18 illuminators, 12 book-binders, 11 parchment-makers, 23 scribes, and 9 stationers and samplers are known to have traded in and around Catte Street in the thirteenth century. It is unlikely that these Oxford numbers represent a typical

Delicate pen sketches were drawn with watery ink before the colours were applied, and fine drawing by one artist was often obliterated by cruder routine work of less expert craftsmen.

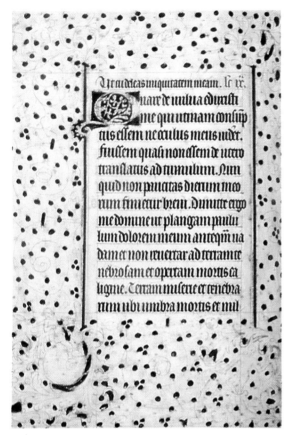

relative proportion between each trade, and it is probably fair to assume that the output of one scribe could keep several illuminators busy. The earlier Winchester records would seem to be about the right balance.

The stages in making an illumination follow much the same order as in the time of St Columba or Charlemagne. The exemplar would be there still, although now commonly provided by a stationer, and the incentive was money rather than the spiritual rewards prepared for in a cold island cell.

The first step was to sketch out with a lead point or scriber the rough outline or composition of the figure or letter. This would be followed by a careful but still faint pen sketch, drawing in specific details of the figures or features, or the intertwining of a decorative letter. The next step was to lay down the size for gilding, which might be made from a variety of substances: the glair mixtures of earlier centuries, or the chalk- or plaster-based preparations of the later Middle Ages. The gold came first because surplus gold leaf tends to stick to any painted surface: and it is interesting to find that even when they used yellow paint as a substitute for gold, the artists of the *Book of Kells* still followed what must already have been a traditional procedure and put the yellow in first.

After the base of size had set, carefully cut pieces of thinly beaten gold

An unfinished 15th-century manuscript at various stages of completion gives an idea of some of the working methods used by the scribes. The production of books was often shared between several workshops.

87

The Application of Gold

Much of the brilliant gold on the initials and background in manuscript books consists of a very thin layer of leaf burnished on to a cushion of gesso – a mixture of plaster, sugar, lead and size – which is laid on the page, and dries slightly raised from its surface. The gesso must be flexible enough to bend with the page without cracking, and when mixed with water or glair to flow freely in a pen.

A typical gesso recipe is: sixteen parts of slaked plaster, six parts of white lead, two parts of powdered sugar, one part of glue, and a dash of colour.

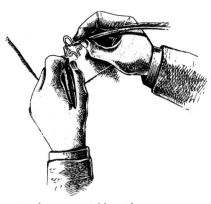

1. Apply gesso quickly with a pen or brush, and leave a slightly domed shape, like a drop of water on glass.

2. When gesso dries, scrape it smooth with a knife, being careful not to flatten the domed effect.

3. Cut gold leaf into convenient pieces, to avoid waste.

4. If the air is insufficiently humid to encourage the gold to stick, breath through a tube onto the surface of the design to increase its dampness.

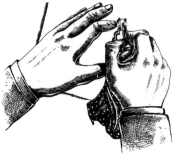

5. Pick up gold leaf and press onto the gesso with a burnishing tool made of polished stone, such as agate or haematite, set into a handle. Press gold firmly down over the design, uniting it with the gesso. Use silk to clean the burnisher.

6. Clean excess gold off the neighbouring writing surface with knife or soft brush.

leaf were laid over it, and burnished on to its surface with a polished stone, usually agate or haematite, or with a shaped animal tooth set into a handle. The effect of the burnishing was to bring to life all the shimmering brilliance of the gold; and the word illumination derives from the effect created by the play of light on a turning gilded page.

We have described the surface that suits the scribe for writing – the slightly raised nap, into which the pen scrapes a slight furrow for the ink to fill – and how this process is conducive to the drawing of fine lines. But the napped surface rejects the softer stroke of the paint-filled brush, as velvet would. To overcome this difficulty, after the pen drawing was completed the painter would sometimes polish down the surface before laying in the background colours. Unfinished books often reveal an astounding indifference to neatness at this stage. Even books with exquisite workmanship on the completed pages seem to start off "badly". The illuminators of course had a practical attitude to their work, and knew that each succeeding layer of detail would conceal the haste of the undercoats. The paler colours first, and step by step brighter and then heavier colours; outlines in black or dark brown added with a pen or brush; and finally the thin highlights on the figures or foliage were added with a fine ermine brush, or even the pin feather from the wing of a bird dipped in white lead paint giving the final sparkle.

On vellum the hard quill pen draws fine lines more effectively than the soft hairs of a brush.

Robert Brekeling's contract with the Dean and Chapter of York Minster in 1346, it will be remembered, stipulated that the first letter to the verses of the psalms should be in "good" blue. Not only did they recognise that the qualities of pigments varied, but the client as well as the craftsman must have had an intimate enough knowledge of the materials involved to be able to judge. There is no doubt that the problem of procuring the right sort of colours, and their cost, must have been a major preoccupation for the medieval illuminators. When we look at those pages dancing with gold and colour we see the outcome of considerable expertise in the preparation of colours. Modern paints without modification cannot reproduce the same effect. The quality and vibrancy required much more careful preparation than squeezing a tube or opening a paintbox. Each colour would be ground, or the dyes mixed, and bound with a medium of egg-yolk, egg-white or gelatin such as parchment size. A well-made painting with egg is as nearly permanent as any kind of painting mankind has yet invented, and paintings in egg tempera have generally changed less in five hundred years than some oil-paintings have in thirty.

Each colour has different properties. Some of the earth colours are literally muddy and thick in the brush or pen. Mercuric sulphide, the vermilion red of the initial letters, on the other hand, flows freely because of its density and covering power. Azurite never likes to forget that however finely ground it may be it is composed of granular little crystals, and using it is like writing or painting with ground glass. Each pigment or glaze needed subtly different handling techniques.

Minium, red sulphide of mercury, also called cinnabar, which the scribes had used since Egyptian times for rubrics, capital letters or headings, gives us the word miniature. The person who worked with

Making an Illuminated Letter

The letter B, shown left, is taken from the Worms Bible, made in the Rhine area of Germany about 1148. On the opposite page it has been copied with its parts at various stages of completion, to show the nine operations involved in making the original. The facsimile can easily be traced, and by following the stages described below anyone can produce his own illuminated letter.

1. Having traced the original, transfer it on to the writing surface with pencil.
2. Sketch the outline with pen and ink.
3. Put down gold size (in this case gum ammoniac) or gold paint.
4. Apply gold leaf to size if used.
5. Apply the palest colours, of which four are identified here.
6. Apply the second layer of colour, the middle tones of pink, green and blue.
7. Add a final coat of each separate colour.
8. Outline the letter with a fine black pen, and complete the black lettering.
9. Finish with fine white hairlines, applied with pen or brush.

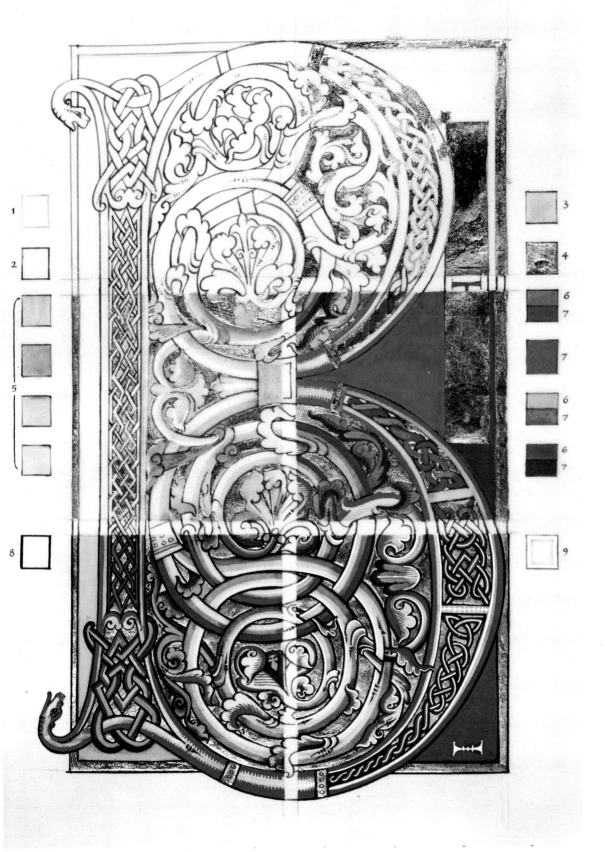

A lay artist is drawing with pen and ink, while a monk supervises his work. This manuscript, made in Paris *c.* 1235, was produced by men working in five separate workshops.

minium was called a miniator, and the things he was to miniate were called miniatures, whether they were tiny or not. In Roman times cinnabar was so precious that it was imported from Spain under seal, with a sale price fixed by law to prevent it becoming impossibly expensive.

Saffron, dyers' herbs and deadly nightshade, buckthorn, malachite ochres and realgar—all needed special knowledge, separate treatment and a skilful and delicate touch in application. It took huge quantities of the tiny whelk to produce a small amount of the purple dye used on the skins of early manuscripts (the Tyrian purple); but as Aldhelm pointed out in a seventh-century riddle, unlike the nasty columbine at least you could eat them too.

> *From twin shells in the blue sea I was born,*
> *And my hairy body turns soft wool*
> *A tawny red. Lo, gorgeous robes I give,*
> *And of my flesh provide men food besides;*
> *A double tribute thus I pay to fate.*

We can judge from the number of books which have survived that the production of and demand for handwritten books must have enormously increased between 1150 and 1450. Diebold Lauber of Hagenau in Alsace ran a veritable book-factory which specialised in "light reading", with illustrations tediously repeated in like vein. By the turn of the thirteenth century books were exported in quantity from Italy to France and England, some in sheets for local finishing. An original note in a French manuscript of about 1450 indicates what might happen to such a book when it was imported; after it was written it would pass through at least ten pairs of hands:

> he who decorated the margins with filigree work
> who illuminated the initials
> who made the pictures
> who made up the gatherings and rubbed them smooth
> who sewed them
> who gilded the leaves
> who made the studs for the cover
> who made the bindings
> who gilded them
> who set them (bosses and boards) in place

In order to obtain some idea of how well the craftsman was paid in the Middle Ages we need some satisfactory method of comparing the value of money in those times with our own. Such comparisons are never clear, because the value attached to goods and to different types of work, and the status of individuals in society, was so very different. We can get some impression of the status of different trades by examining the tax lists of Paris in 1292, where different tradesmen were taxed according to the value of their possessions. There were over 15,000 taxpayers in Paris in that year, of whom only 33 were painters, 24 were image-makers, and 13 were illuminators. Understandably, they were greatly outnumbered by people who made their living providing rather more essential necessities of life: there were over 350 shoemakers, and just as many who made clothes. 104 made patisseries and sweetmeats, and 157 kept eating-houses and taverns. The richest Parisians, needless to say, were the Lombard bankers and financiers. Amongst tradesmen and craftsmen the most highly taxed were two potters who ranked with merchants of precious and semi-precious stones; and two mercers (dealers in costly textiles) paid much the same. A great many others paid between five and ten livres, but only one painter, called Nicholas, managed to reach this class by being taxed six livres. After him the level drops rapidly to two painters and an image-maker, who paid little more than one livre, and the rest of the craftsmen paid less than half that sum. Even the most distinguished book illuminator of his time, Master Honoré, some of whose books produced for the court survive to this day and are of the highest standard of skill and technical mastery, paid a mere ten sous in tax. Although he may have lived comfortably, his taxation level provides concrete evidence that his pay in comparison with other trades at the time was low.

In the 1320s a French scholar, Jean de Jandun, wrote a treatise in praise of Paris in which he included a chapter on the manual artificers who worked there. Jostling with the bakers and the fashioners of metal vessels, the book producers' existence is recorded with approval: "The more intently the parchment-makers, scribes, illuminators and book-binders devote themselves in the service of wisdom to the decoration of their work, the more copiously do the delightful fountains of knowledge flow forth from that most profound source of all good things.''

The craftsmen and artists were also low on the social ladder. Even if the excellence of their work brought them to the notice of the rich and powerful, it was not enough – unless they had something else to offer – to earn them a place at court. Jack of St Albans, painter of King Edward II in 1326, was paid a sum of money "for dancing before the king upon a table"; and even an artist of the standing of Giotto would not have enjoyed so close an association with royalty if he had been a less interesting personality. The Limbourg brothers, on the other hand, illuminators to the greatest of all French patrons of medieval book art, the Duc de Berry, seem to have managed skilfully to combine business with amity, and enjoyed a close relationship with their patron. They must also have been well paid, for one of them was able to lend the duke

Right. A stationer's shop (Bologna, 15th century). Bundles of quills are displayed outside, while work proceeds within. One man is erasing writing from a sheet of vellum for re-use, while another is trimming sheets to size. *Opposite.* Biblical scenes are illustrated with the figures wearing contemporary dress and armour. The marginal notes are in Arabic and Hebrew.

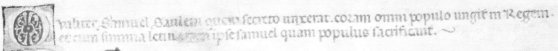

aliter. Samuel. Dauiem quem fecreto unxerat. coram omni populo ungit in Regem. et cum summa letitia tam ipse samuel quam populus sacrificant.

a large sum of money in 1415; but not everyone in his service was so lucky. Poor Drouet de Dammartin, the mason, died in 1413 owed as much as fourteen years back pay by the same illustrious prince. The astute Limbourgs had known their man well enough to exact security in the form of a ruby. Another illuminator working for Philip "the Good" of Burgundy, after serving his prince for a lifetime, was reduced to beggary because of non-payment. And Henri Bellechose, appointed official painter to Philip, went unpaid for fourteen years and his wife had to help out by running a market stall. No one could blame the gifted artists who decided to join a religious community and work peacefully in the security of the cloisters.

Of course, not all of the work carried out in the scriptoria of the monasteries or by the commercial scribes in the cities reached a uniform standard of excellence. Much of it was routine and mediocre, and a good deal of it thoroughly incompetent. As in all fields of human endeavour only the smallest amount of work reaches the peaks of artistry and excellence. On the whole, the best that could be hoped for, then as now, was that the job should be well done. The art, for the most part, was a by-product.

In the great Gothic cathedrals built throughout Europe at this time the lettering carved into their stones was relegated to a very minor role. Gone was the confident sophistication of the letter carvers who had made the stately capitals in marble or inlaid in bronze which had swaggered proudly across the triumphal arches and cornices of Rome. The medieval carvers of Cluny, for example, made shapes which owed more to the daintiness of pen-made letters on the page of a book than to the swelling spread of a chisel-edged brush.

An important source of income for the scribe in many cities was the production of official texts for students in the new universities and schools; and no doubt some of them succeeded in exploiting their young customers. In 1265 an anxious father wrote to a friend, "I told my son, 'Go to Paris or Bologna and I will send you £100 a year'; and what did the boy do? He went to Paris and had his books made to prattle with gold letters!"

In the early days of the universities the curriculum was limited and a wide range of texts was not needed; and the long-lasting parchment books could be used again and again by succeeding generations of students. University libraries as such were not created until later on in the Middle Ages, although some libraries in Paris were given specific bequests to provide books for the use of poor students, "for as long as they last". A rich young man would commission his own specially illuminated "prattling" copies, complete with his own coat of arms, direct from the stationer, but few were so fortunate. A poor student in the universities of Oxford or Bologna could only write out his own texts laboriously letter by letter. He would borrow one chapter or gathering at a time from the specially licensed university stationer, who kept un-bound sections of approved texts for hire. In this way several students could copy from the same book, each in his own room, using quills on pages of sheepskin bought from the parchmenter, or ready made up in

The carved letters which accompanied the sculptures on the great Gothic cathedrals often owed more to the influence of the quill than to the brush-inspired letter forms of ancient Rome. Cluny Abbey, late 11th century. *Overleaf.* The humanist scholars of the wealthy Italian city states created a demand for books decorated and written in a style which reflected their romantic view of the ancient Roman past. They rejected the northern blackletter in favour of the lighter and more spacious forms of the Carolingian book hand, which they renamed *antiqua.*

blank books from the stationer.

The licensed stationer was required to display in his shop a list of the *exemplaria* which he held, the number of pieces it contained and the official price for hiring them. It is hardly surprising that many of the books thus copied by the students were written in an extremely hurried fashion, in tiny handwriting with the maximum amount of abbreviation. Some have survived, and they are excessively dog-eared. This demanding system was used in many of the European universities, including Paris, Bologna, Oxford, Naples and Padua.

The same principles which created the earliest writing in the river plains of Sumeria still played their part in shaping the outward form of letters in the fifteenth century. The Sumerians had used available

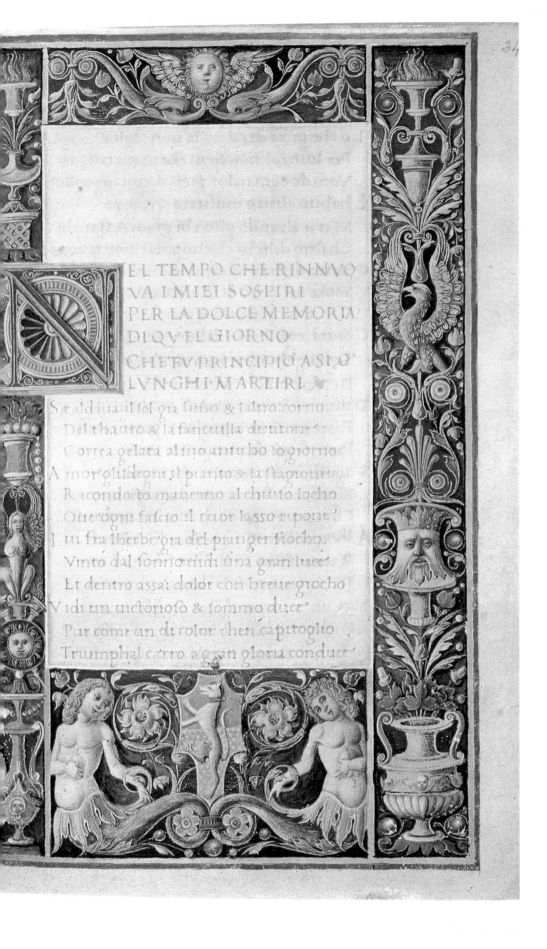

EL TEMPO CHE RINNVO
VA I MIEI SOSPIRI
PER LA DOLCE MEMORIA
DI QVEL GIORNO
CHE FV PRINCIPIO A SI O
LVNGHI MARTIRI

Scaldaua il sol gia luno & laltro corno
Del thauro & la fanciulla de titone
Correa gelata al suo antico soggiorno
Amor gli sdegni il pianto & la stagione
Ricondocto maueano al chiuso locho
Oue ogni fascio il cuor lasso ripone
Iui fra lherbe gia del pianger fiocho
Vinto dal sonno uidi una gran luce
Et dentro assai dolor con breue giocho
Vidi un uictorioso & sommo duce
Pur come un di color chen capitoglio
Triumphal carro a gran gloria conduce

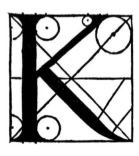

materials and technology—clay tablets and sticks to make symbols which echo sounds—and the evolution and influence of their system depended on their success as a power in the world. The rounded urbanity of the Carolingian minuscule, which had survived and circulated through the needs of the cloister, was altered and adapted to the new needs of a commercial, secular and political world, becoming the compressed, economical, no-nonsense style we call Gothic.

While much of Europe had been decimated by the Black Death and exhausted by endless wars and dynastic quarrels throughout the fourteenth century, the merchant princes of Lombardy were working to create a new technology, that of international finance. In the wealthy city states of Italy a nostalgia for the past, which so easily could have been self-indulgent and debilitating, turned instead into a vigorous and revitalising current which inspired writers, artists and craftsmen to give expression to the new mood, the new Renaissance. The poet, Petrarch, who had done much to inspire renewed interest in the glories of the ancient world, wrote:

> *The very sight of men of the present time wounds me sorely, whereas the memories, the deeds, and the illustrious names of the ancients, give me joy, splendid and so inestimable that, if the world could know, it would be amazed that I should have so much pleasure in talking with the dead and so little with the living.*

In the regions of northern Italy dominated by the republics of Florence and Venice the new learning flourished and began to spread. No doubt it was not the professional scribes who took the lead in innovation. Like the gentleman-inventors in eighteenth- and nineteenth-century industrial societies, who paid local craftsmen to carry out their ideas, it was the amateur scholar-scribes of Florence who had to teach and encourage the professionals in the new style which their studies had inspired. The scholars and patrons of Florence and Venice were turning their backs on the Gothic chill of northern Europe.

In the early fifteenth century there was a burst of scholarship in the field of classical studies; and already around 1400 the scholar-scribe Poggio Bracciolini had begun to revise his own book-hand. He based it on the Carolingian minuscule, not only on the original ninth-century script of Aachen and Tours, but also on eleventh- or twelfth-century Italian versions which had developed before being overtaken by the compression of the succeeding centuries. The current book-hand of the early 1400s was *Rotunda*, or *Italian Gothic*. It was slightly more curvaceous, as its name suggests, than its northern counterparts, but it was still unmistakably a member of the Gothic family. Poggio's revived Carolingian script became known as "littera antiqua", to distinguish it from the current Italian Gothic book-hand which was also known as "littera moderna". Books in the new script were soon sought after by collectors, and it spread rapidly to other centres of learning in Italy, where it was principally used for the copying of classical texts. Scribes trained in the new humanist styles (but no doubt also competent in the older legal and book-hands) moved from city to city, where patrons like the kings of

Naples and the dukes of Lombardy were willing to pay high prices for the skills of calligraphy and illumination with which to stock their libraries.

The stationers, as they did in Paris and Oxford, prospered in Florence. Vespasiano da Bisticci, who was well connected with rich and aristocratic patrons, acted as a middle man, arranging for the production of books that might be written in Florence, decorated in Rome and sold for use in a royal library in Naples. The same scribes seem also, at least in Florence, to have acted as notaries.

The romance of revivalism produced plenty of eccentric characters, like the artist, Felice Feliciano, who combined picnic outings with hunting for classical inscriptions which he copied from ruined monuments in the Italian countryside. By the mid-fifteenth century the style which had been developed by amateur scholars and aesthetes of this kind had become widely exploited as a commercial book-hand by the professionals. Florence continued to dominate this trade until well into the third quarter of the fifteenth century. After a formal beginning, the rounded and separately-formed Carolingian letters became subject to cursive tendencies, no doubt in the interests of speed and economy; and alongside them emerged a cursive version which before long became accepted as a style in its own right, the style we now call *Italic*.

The days of the professional scribe-copyist were now numbered. Even as early as 1457, when Vespasiano the stationer was employing as many as 50 scribes at a time, a group of men in Germany were peeling off a hundred vellum pages an hour from their new printing press.

Above. A scribe's workshop in the early 16th century. Note the hourglass on the desk. *Opposite.* The Renaissance writing masters attempted to reconstruct classical inscriptions by dogmatic systems based on geometry alone.

7. The Scribe and the Printer

A page from the first psalter ever printed with moveable type, Mainz, 1457. The blue and red used on the initial letter B are thought to have been made from special interlocking blocks separately inked, but printed with the black.

The earliest experiments in printing in Europe involved transferring a calligrapher's designs, in reverse, on to the surface of a smooth wooden block, cutting away the wood surrounding the letter-shapes, and applying printing ink to the remaining surface of the letters. Paper or vellum could then be pressed downwards on to the inked block, which transferred the black shapes of the letters on to its white surface.

After the initial labour of engraving a whole page of text on to a single wooden block in this way, many identical copies could be reproduced with little effort or further expense. From that simple beginning came the idea of using interchangeable letters carved into separate small blocks of wood, with the advantage that the letters could be re-used again and again in different combinations. But it was extremely laborious to hand-carve the enormous number of units which were required to supply all the pages of set type needed to print a whole book at one time.

Johannes Gutenberg was born in the 1390s and was a member of the goldsmiths' guild in Mainz. He had become fascinated by the idea of reproducing by mechanical means the richly decorated handwritten manuscripts of his day, and embarked in secret on experiments to produce solutions to the problems involved. As a metalsmith he naturally thought in terms of manufacturing type in metal, by analogy with the metalsmiths' traditional techniques of casting and punching. A goldsmiths' trademark or initials were commonly engraved into a hard metal punch, which was then struck into the soft gold or silver leaving an identical impression time after time.

The technique used for casting was to pour molten metal into a prepared mould in which the design had previously been carved. By carefully engraving the letters of the alphabet on to punches, and striking them into a soft piece of brass placed at the bottom of a narrow and adjustable wooden mould, hundreds of identical lead sticks with perfect reproductions of the letter punch's impressions could be manufactured with ease and precision.

Lead alone was too soft, however, to stand the continual pressure of a printing press, and a special alloy had to be developed which was neither too soft nor too hard and brittle. The right inks had to be found, and better presses devised. Gutenberg borrowed money from a lawyer acquaintance, Johannes Fust, to enable him to continue his experiments, which by this time had aroused considerable curiosity as well as attempts at industrial espionage.

Whether a large reading public would exist for printed books could not be foreseen, and the first attempts were to produce luxury editions which might compete with the attractions of handwritten and illumi-

Regē magnū dūm venite adoꝛemus, ꝓs Uenite.
Oñicas diebꝫ poſt teſtū epħie Inuitatoꝛiū·

Adoꝛemꝰ dūm qui fecit nos, Oꝭ vnite aū Seruite·

eatus vir qui
non abiịt in
conſilio impioꝛū et in
via pccõꝛ nõ ſtetit: ꝛ in
cathedra peſtilēcie nõ ſe=
dit, Sed ī lege dūi vo
lūtas ei⁹: et in lege eūis meditabiꞇ die ac
nocte, Et erit tanꝗ lignū qđ plātatū iſte
ſecꝰ decurſus aꝗꝛ: qđ fru ctū ſuū dabit ĩ
tꝥ ſuo Et foliū ei⁹ nõ defluet: ꝛ oīa ꝗcūꝗ
faciet ꝓſperabūꞇ, Nõ ſic impị nõ ſic ſed
tanꝗ puluis quē picit vntꝰ a facie terre,
Ideo non reſurgīꞇ impị in iudicio: neꝗ
pctõꝛes in cõſilio iuſtoꝛ Qū nouit dūs
via iuſtoꝛ: ꝛ iter impioꝛ pribit, Gka P

Evovae·

nated books. The printer sought to emulate the scribe's skill and dexterity, and spaces were still left for the illuminator to complete the pages in the traditional manner.

It may well have been that Gutenberg became too engrossed in the technical problems of reproducing these elaborate initial letters; for after even more money had been advanced to him by his backer, Fust became infuriated by the delays and by what he considered to be the inventor's unworldly preoccupation with perfection. Just as he was about to publish his first works, a Bible and a psalter, Fust took legal action against him in 1445, and he was stripped of all his equipment and type. Before long his old partner put this to use, and when in 1457 the first book to be printed in Europe which carried the printer's name was published, it bore not Gutenberg's imprint but that of Fust and his son-in-law Peter Schöffer, who had been Gutenberg's apprentice and assistant and had been a witness against him at his trial. Financially ruined, Gutenberg died in poverty within ten years – but not before he had seen others make their fortunes from his ideas.

The techniques developed by Gutenberg and his associates were a fusion of ideas from many sources, some of them ancient. Paper, for example, had been invented as early as 100 AD in China, and had found its way to Europe via the Arab world and twelfth-century Spain. The ink was developed from Flemish techniques of oil painting with pigments ground in linseed oil varnish. The arts of the metalsmith were employed to find practicable casting techniques for type and a suitable alloy of antimony, tin and lead. The printing presses constructed by Gutenberg were also based on traditional principles used in the olive-oil and paper-making trades.

The new printing trade soon flourished, and within ten years of the appearance of the first printed psalter in Mainz German and Dutch craftsmen had spread printing throughout Europe. The principal export from Germany was not books but technology. Craftsmen trained in German printing shops took their skills to every country in western Christendom, and printing shops opened in Cologne, Basel, Paris, Valencia, Seville, Naples, and all the great centres of trade, banking and shipping, and the seats of political and ecclesiastical authority. Italy was a prime area of expansion for adventurous printers, where a buoyant economy and the spreading Renaissance culture of humanism provided them with far more opportunity than in the still largely cloistered and medieval German society.

These printer-craftsmen took with them the type punches and letter designs modelled on the Gothic black-letter provided originally by their local scribes. The first press to be set up outside Germany was in 1465 in the Benedictine Abbey of Subiaco near Rome, and significantly those disciplined columns of black Gothic text-letters did not long survive the rapid march over the Alps unchallenged. Although the first book to be printed in Italy, less than ten years after the Mainz psalter, was the work of two German craftsmen, Conrad Sweynheym and Arnold Pannartz, its design from the very start was unmistakably in the Italian humanist style. The minuscule letters of Charlemagne had found their way into

Johannes Gutenberg.

Right. The specimen sheet of Erhard Ratdolt, dated 1 April 1486 in Augsburg, but probably printed in Venice. The heavier type-style is based on the traditional Italian book hand derived from the *rotunda* script.

ue maria
gr̄a plena
dominus
tecū bene
dicta tu in mulierib'
et benedictus fruct'
uentris tui : ihesus
christus amen.

Gloria laudis resonet in ore
omniū Patri genitoqꝪ proli
spiritui sancto pariter Resul
tet laude perhenni Labori
bus dei vendunt nobis om
nia bona. laus: honor: virtus
potētia: ꝯ gratiaꝝ actio tibi
christe. Amen.

Uiue deū sic ꝯ viues per secula cun
cta. Prouidet ꝯ tribuit deus omnia
nobis. Proficit absque deo null⁹ in
orbe labor. Illa placet tell⁹ in qua
res parua beatū. Oe facit ꝯ tenues
luxuriantur opes.

Si fortuna volet fies de rhetore consul.
Si volet hec eadem fies de cōsule rhetor.
Quicquid amor iussit nó est cōtédere tutū
Regnat et in dominos ius habet ille suos
Hi ra data é vt ꝝ da data é sine fenere nobis
Mutua: nec certa persoluenda die.

Usus ꝯ ars docuit quod sapit omnis homo
Ars animos frangit ꝯ firmas dirimit vrbes
Arte cadunt turres arte leuatur onus
Artibus ingenijs quesita est gloria multis
Principijs obsta sero medicina paratur
Cum mala per longas conualuere moras
Sed propera nec te venturas differ in horas
Qui non est hodie cras minus aptus erit.

Non bene pro toto libertas venditur auro
Hoc celeste bonum preterit orbis opes
Precuncta animi est bonis veneranda liberras
Seruitus semper cunctis quoque despicienda
Summa petit liuor perflant altissima uenti
Summa petunt dextra fulmina missa iouis
In loca nonnunquam siccis arentia glebis
Be prope currenti flumine man at aqua

Quisquis ades scriptis qui mentem forsitan istis
Ut noscas adhibes protinus istud opus
Nosce: augustensis ratdolt germanus Erhardus
Litterulas istos ordine quasqꝪ facit
Ipse quibus veneta libros impressit in vrbe
Multos ꝯ plures nunc premit atqꝪ premet
Ouique etiam varijs celestia signa figuris
Aurea qui primus nunc monumenta premit
Quin etiam manibus propijs vbicunqꝪ figuras
Est opus: incidens dedalus alter erit

Nobis benedicat qui i trinitate vinit
ꝯ regnat Amen: Honor soli deo est tribuendū
Aue regina celoꝝ mater regis angelo
rum o maria flos virginum velut rosa
velilium o maria : Tua est potentia tu
rt gnius domine tu es super omnes gen
tes da pacem domine in dieb⁹ nostris
mirabilis deus in sanctis suis Et glori
osus in maiestate sua oth panthon kyr

Quod prope sacce diem tibi sum conuiua futurus
forsitan ignoras at fore ne dubites
Ergo para cenam non qualem stoicus ambit
Sed lautam sane more cirenaico
Nanque duas mecum florente etate puellas
Adducam quarum balsama cinnus olet
Uernula sola domi sedeat quam nuper habebas
Si nondum cunnus vepribus horruerit
Sunt qui insimulent ꝯ auari crimen amici
O biciant facto rumor utiste cadat   Hec Philelphus

Nunc adeas mira quicunqꝪ uolumina queris
Arte uel er animo pressa fuisse tuo
Seruiet iste tibi: nobis iure sorores
Incolumem seruet usqꝪ rogare licet

Est homini uirtus fuluo preciosior auro: ænæas
Ingenium quondam fuerat preciosius auro.
MiramurqꝪ magis quos munera mentis adornát:
Quam qui corporeis emicuere bonis.
Si qua uirtute nites ne despice quenquam
Ex alia quadam forsitan ipse nitet

Nemo sue laudis nimium letetur honore
Ne uilis factus post sua fata gemat.
Nemo nimis cupide sibi res desiderat ullas
Ne dum plus cupiat perdat & id quod habet.
Ne ue cito uerbis cuiusquam credito blandis
Sed si sint fidei respice quid moneant
Qui bene proloquitur coram sed postea praue
Hic erit inuisus bina qꝪ ora gerat

Pax plenam uirtutis opus pax summa laborum
pax belli exacti præcium est præciumque pericli
Sidera pace uigent consistunt terrea pace
Nil placitum sine pace deo non munus ad aram
Fortuna arbitriis tempus dispensat ubi
Illa rapit iuuenes illa ferit senes

κλιω Τευτερπη τε θαλεία τε μελπομενη τε
τεφψιχορη τερατω τε πολυμνεία τουρανιη
τε καλλιοπη θέΔη προφερεςατη εξ ινατα
σαωψ   ιεσυο χριςουο μαρια   τελοσ.

Indicis characteꝝ diuersaꝝ mane
rierū impressioni paratarū: Finis.

Erhardi Ratdolt Augustensis viri
solertissimi: preclaro ingenio ꝯ miri
fica arte: qua olim Venetijs excelluit
celebratissimus. In imperiali nunc
vrbe Auguste vindelicoꝝ laudatissi
me impressioni dedit. AnnoqꝪ salu
tis. M.LLLL.LXXXVI. Kal̄.
Aprilis Sidere felici compleuit.

P·VIRGILII MARO
NIS GEORGICON
LIBER·I·
AD MECAENATEM·
VID FAC
AT LAE
TAS SE
GETES
QVO SIDERE TERRĀ

Vertere mecænas : ulmisq. adiungere uites
Conueniat : quæ cura boum : quis cultus habendo

print for the first time.

Venice in the fifteenth century, the "Pearl of the Adriatic", was still the leading trading city in the world, and the first printing press was opened there in 1467 by two Rhenish brothers, Johann and Wendelin of Speier. Its first production, an edition of three hundred copies in Roman type of Cicero's *Epistolae ad familiares*, sold out immediately. They reprinted, and in the second printing Johann was able to proclaim with understandable pride:

> *From Italy once each German bought a book.*
> *A German now will give more than they took.*
> *For John, a man whom few in skill surpass,*
> *Has shown that books may best be writ in brass.*

For the first thirty years after printing became established in Italy and elsewhere in Europe, the printers strictly followed the conventions of handwritten books; and it was not surprising, since the basis of legibility is familiarity, that their potential customers would have found any new-fangled design difficult to accept. The new process of book-production was not always welcomed on aesthetic grounds either. The cosmopolitan Federigo, Duke of Urbino, who would not attach great importance to the relative cheapness and easier availability of printed books since he could afford manuscripts, refused to have any such unworthy mass-produced objects in the same library as his beautiful collection of handwritten and decorated texts. Nonetheless the first printed books in the Gutenberg tradition were hardly cheap; it has been calculated that one Bible alone used over 300 skins of parchment.

In more expensive printed books spaces were still left in the text for the illuminator to add his finishing touches, and some printers, like Gutenberg before them, continued to chase moonbeams by imitating flourishes in the handwritten manner, and evolved elaborate decorated capitals to accompany the text. Type does not lend itself to a slavish imitation of calligraphy. Gutenberg had needed over three hundred individual letters and abbreviations to reproduce the "feel" of a handwritten page. Individual clusters of letters had to be carved joined together by ligatures in order to imitate the natural joins of writing with a quickly moving quill pen.

This manuscript of Virgil was probably written and decorated by Bartholomeo San Vito of Padua between 1497 and 1499. The lower case letters used at the foot of the page show clear links with the Carolingian style; while the capital Q, whose troublesome tail has been sawn off and placed out of harm's way, is an imitation of the V-cut letters of 1st-century Rome. In his technique for ruling guidelines, the scribe has reverted to the blind scoring method of earlier times.

As a new generation became familiar with the printed book—and by the last quarter of the fifteenth century there were as many as a hundred and fifty printing presses established in Venice alone—physical changes in the appearance of the handmade letters began to appear, influenced by the process of simplification and economy and by the punch-cutter's special skills. The closely woven text of the calligrapher began to give way to the open and aloof practicality of separated letters. The act of engraving the image of a letter into the steel of the type-cutter's punch with a pointed engraving tool is totally unlike the quick, scurrying action of a square-cut goose quill. It has much more in common with the process of carving letters in stone. And indeed the new letter shapes began to resemble the incised letters carved into the marble monuments of Rome as far back as the first century AD. They retained a fairly strong

Right. A self-portrait of Juan de Yciar, from the title page of his book *Arte subtilissima* (1548). *Below.* The anchor and dolphin in Aldus Manutius' printer's mark symbolise the motto *festina lente*, "hasten slowly".

family likeness to the calligraphy of the humanist scribes, but in detail they were influenced by the punch-cutter's burin or engraving tool.

Great numbers of books were printed in Venice in the 1470s. The Speier brothers were succeeded by another foreigner, Nicholas Jensen, a Frenchman who produced some 150 books around this time. It was Aldus Manutius, however, who first saw that there was a market for smaller books in pocket editions, scholarly but compact, handy and cheap. Instead of printing only a few hundred copies at a time he printed a thousand. And in order to find a more compressed and economical type-face he turned to the cursive Italic script of the humanist scribes, in collaboration with a gifted type-designer, Francesco Griffo, who based his fount on the *Cancellaresca Corsiva* of the papal chancery.

Aldus Manutius was the greatest entrepreneur publisher of his time, and he chose this lovely Italic type, and others, entirely on strict practical criteria. By his efforts and the prestige which his publications enjoyed, the "antique" humanist types of Jensen and Griffo finally ousted the black-letter type almost everywhere in Europe. But not all printed books reached the standard or enjoyed the reputation of the Aldine imprint. Other establishments sometimes did a very poor job. A 172-page book made in a monastic workshop in 1561 was found by the editor to contain so many errors that the list of corrections was fifteen pages long. The editor assigned the blunders to the devil's work: somehow the manuscript seems to have been soaked in a kennel before reaching the printer, who no doubt reading it at arm's length was induced to make a great many errors in setting the type.

At first after the arrival of the printed book the artist-scribes and illuminators remained quite prosperous. For centuries their principal clients had been wealthy private patrons who collected their work as much for its artistic content as for the substance of the text. There was still work for the illuminators, decorating and hand-finishing the printed pages. Chancery scribes were unaffected because legal, diplomatic and religious documents and letters, being by their nature one-off productions, continued to be handwritten. And for a time the sumptuous books in the Renaissance style, and even *editions de luxe* from the Low

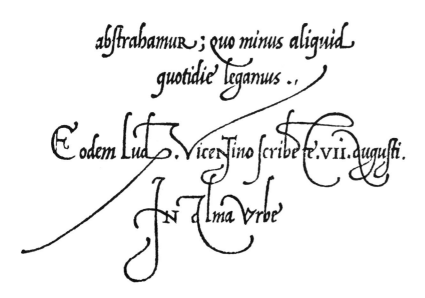

abstrahamur; quo minus aliquid quotidie legamus

Eodem Lud. Vicentino scribe̅te. VII. augusti.

In alma vrbe

A detail from the first printed copybook of its kind, by Arrighi, published at Rome in 1522. *Below.* A printer's workshop. In the foreground one man inks the type with felt-covered leather pads, while the other lays paper onto it before sliding the bed underneath the press. Working in this way two men could print up to 120 pages an hour. In the background, a typesetter fills his stick, reading from the copy before him.

Countries, reached new heights of technical perfection and artistry. Yet even so the distinguished scribe Antonio Sinibaldi felt the pinch sufficiently to plead poverty when filling in his tax form in 1480, claiming that he had lost so much copying work on account of the invention of printing that he could hardly afford to clothe himself.

The size of the reading public, and thus the market for those who wished to instruct others in the arts of reading and writing, was greatly enlarged by the arrival of the printed book. In 1522 Ludovico Arrighi

Psalmus

Misereremei dñs
secundum ma
gnam misericor.

De sancto Joanne.

Inter natos mulierum non surrexit maior Joan
ne baptista qui viam domino preparauit. Fuit homo
missus a deo cui nomen erat Joannes. &c.

Πάτερ ἡμῶν ὁ ἐν τοῖς οὐρανοῖς, ἁγιασθήτω
τὸ ὄνομά σου· ἐλθέτω ἡ βασιλεία σου· γε-
νηθήτω τὸ θέλημά σου, ὡς ἐν οὐρανῷ
καὶ ἐπὶ τῆς γῆς· τὸν ἄρτον ἡμῶν τὸν ἐ-
πιούσιον δὸς ἡμῖν σήμερον· καὶ ἄφες ἡμῖν
τὰ ὀφειλήματα ἡμῶν, ὡς καὶ ἡμεῖς ἀ-
φίεμεν τοῖς ὀφειλέταις ἡμῶν· καὶ μὴ
εἰσενέγκῃς ἡμᾶς εἰς πειρασμόν, ἀλλὰ ῥῦσαι
ἡμᾶς ἀπὸ τοῦ πονηροῦ. Ἀμήν.

A 19th-century recon-
struction of William
Caxton's workshop, as he
shows King Edward IV
his new printing press
(Daniel Maclise, 1806–70).
Opposite. A page of
sample scripts, from a
manuscript made for a
rich patron by Francesco
Moro. Italian, *c.* 1565.

published the first printed writing manual, *Operina*, which invited the
public to learn his favoured *cancellaresca* writing style "in a few days";
and over the following fifty years a host of imitators and rival writing-
masters published competing works, notably Tagliente, Palatino, and
Cresci who was appointed scriptor to the Vatican library in 1556. They
were made for a public now familiar with the antique types of the
humanists as well as with the cursive Gothic scripts of the professional
notary, and together with the examples of the papal and diplomatic
documents themselves these styles were disseminated throughout
Europe. Kings, clerks and educated men and women everywhere
imitated the style of the Italian writing-masters, and before long scribes
in other countries were producing copybooks of their own. Caspar Neff
brought out a copybook in Germany in 1549, in Spain Juan de Yciar
published his *Arte subtilissima* (1548), and French and English scribes
followed suit. The humanist cursive script found favour in court circles
along with the "new learning" in England, and Elizabeth I and her
contemporaries were taught to master the Italian chancery hand in their
schoolbooks and letters.

The first writing manuals were not engraved in metal. Although
Arrighi used a goldsmith to engrave his written designs, they were cut
into the surface of a wooden block just as in the early printing experi-

The 16th-century Spanish writing master Andreas Brun published writing sheets with white lettering on a pale background as a teaching aid.

ments. In the artist's design the letters would be drawn in reverse, and on the block the wood surrounding the letter-shapes was cut away, so that the block would print the actual shape of the letter. Sometimes in the copybooks the letters themselves would be cut away, so that the background only would be printed black and the letters appear white. These authors did not confine themselves to the humanist Roman and chancery scripts. Their writing manuals were often crammed with all manner of conceits. As well as the business hands of the counting houses and the court hands of the notaries some included Hebrew, Greek and Arabic, scrollwork alphabets and borders filled with human figures, animals and vegetation. The Spanish writing master Andreas Brun came up with an idea to help and encourage students: his copybooks were printed so that the letters came out white against a background of pale brick-red. The student was then instructed to take a pen of the same width as the white letters, and to write directly on top of them in black ink. If this was done at all neatly the completed page would look extremely handsome, to the great encouragement of the young scribe. Unfortunately, because of this method of instruction very few examples of his exemplars remain; although later he also produced books with a black background and instructed students to lay a thin sheet of paper over each page and trace his letters through it.

There seems to have been considerable competition between the various masters and the merits of their different systems, and even some acrimony. The spiky, prancing angularity of Arrighi's chancery script had its champions then as it does today. It also had its determined detractors, such as Giovanni Francesco Cresci, whose own hand possessed rather more verve and passion. As always a man's character is difficult to conceal once he puts pen to paper.

Unlike Arrighi, Cresci did not claim to teach penmanship in "a few days". In his view each pupil should have a deep and systematic grounding, a daily lesson from the master on five basic elements in the writer's craft—small letter shapes, capitals, joins, abbreviations, and the shaping and cutting of the quill pen—and continual practice and study. His pupils' progress was graded according to ability over a period of six months.

Cresci pointed out that the "old-fashioned" chancery Italic of Tagliente, Vincentino, Arrighi and Palatino was slow; and there was some truth in this because much of the thrust of their letters was in an up-and-down, zigzag movement, as compared with the strong lateral flow of his own writing. Furthermore, the square-cut pen held at an angle moves much less quickly from left to right than the narrower and more pointed pen which he advocated. Cresci's designs were woodblock printed, but he was aware of the limitations of this technique and apologises in one of his books for the fact that the printed letter forms lack the clarity and neatness of his original designs. In the 1560s an improvement in rolling mill techniques allowed printers to work from engraved copper plates, which were large enough and sufficiently uniform in quality to be suitable for the engraving of handwritten scripts, producing a much neater and cleaner line than wood. Cresci nonetheless preferred the old method on the grounds that it was more faithful in spirit to his pen lettering, and complained that the engraver, tracing over the writing with his pointed burin, destroyed the nuances of the original and imposed his own subtle gradation in the line. It is ironical that the very cursive and fluid styles, written with a finely cut and flexible pen, which he used and strenuously advocated in opposition to the classic square-cut-pen script, led the way to the tyranny of exaggerated flourishes and bravura artificiality of the engraved, as opposed to written, copperplate script—a tyranny which was to dominate personal handwriting for the next four hundred years. From now on the writing-masters and their students would have to imitate rather than initiate with their sharply pointed quill pens the sugary flourishes of the engraver's burin.

Paper

Rags make paper
Paper makes money
Money makes banks
Banks make loans
Loans make beggars
Beggars make rags.

Paper can be made from most fibrous vegetable materials. After early experiments with cork, fishnets, mulberry bark and macerated linen rags, the Chinese produced excellent paper from linen fibres alone. After it had been left to rot and break down, the linen was cleaned, bleached and pulped, and then mixed with water and wheat flour paste. This fibre-laden watery soup was scooped from a tub on to a flat, mesh-covered frame so that the surplus water drained away, leaving an even "mat" of interlocking fibres stranded over the upper surface of the mesh. This sheet was then peeled off, pressed and dried.

We do not know exactly when the art of paper-making was invented in China, because its manufacture was for many centuries a most closely

The script of Charlemagne developed into the Italic hands of Arrighi (*above*) and Cresci (*overleaf*).

Overleaf. Luxury volumes produced in Italy were often commissioned by foreigners. This one, with writing attributed to Arrighi, was made about 1520 and later presented to Henry VIII of England.

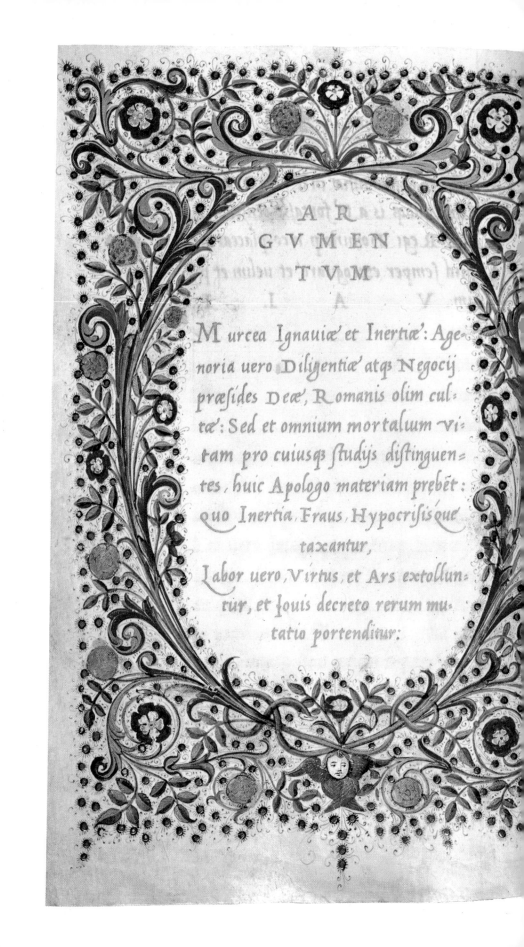

ARGVMENTVM

Murcea Ignauiæ et Inertiæ: Age-
noria uero Diligentiæ atqꝫ Negocij
præsides Deæ, Romanis olim cul-
tæ: Sed et omnium mortalum vi-
tam pro cuiusqꝫ studijs distinguen-
tes, huic Apologo materiam preƀēt:
Quo Inertia, Fraus, Hypocrisisꝗue
taxantur,
Labor uero, Virtus, et Ars extollun-
tur, et Jouis decreto rerum mu-
tatio portenditur:

PANDVLPHI
COLLENVCII PISAVRENSIS
APOLOGVS·
CVI ·TITVLVS
AGENORIA

NER
tiam natu in
ter filias mi
norem, fatuã
alioquin atqʒ
inſtrenuam

fœminam, Sed cui blanda ſpecies atqʒ al
lectrix eſſet, Labori, commum gentium
Deo, Orcus pater vxorem dedit. In
gentes (ut eſt locuples deus) dotis nomi
ne diuitias pollicens, ſi ex ea liberos gi

Above. The script used by Cresci in this letter in 1562 foreshadows the engraved copperplate loops advocated by the writing masters of later centuries.

guarded secret, and its export a lucrative source of income. The probable date is around 100 AD, and for six hundred years the technique was known only inside China.

In 751 AD the Moslem governor of Samarkand is reported to have taken Chinese prisoners, some of whom were skilled paper-makers. According to one version of the story these men set up paper-making shops in the city; but another version claims that they betrayed their secret only under torture. Gradually a knowledge of paper-making techniques spread to other Islamic cities, and its use began to displace parchment for religious texts.

Good quality raw materials for the pulp were always in short supply, however, and in eleventh-century Egypt even the linen wrappings from the graves of embalmed corpses were robbed, and sold to paper factories. By the twelfth century the Arabs had introduced paper to Spain and Sicily, where rags still formed such an important ingredient in the making of pulp that the laws of Alphonso X of Spain in 1236 described the paper as "cloth parchment".

From Sicily the art of paper-making spread to Italy, and Italian craftsmen established it elsewhere in Europe. By 1276 there was paper production at Fabriano, near Ancona; within the next century mills using water-driven hammers to macerate the rotted cotton and linen fibres had been set up all over northern Italy; and soon there were similar mills in Germany and France. By the early fifteenth century even peasants were able to afford linen clothes, and for the first time there was no shortage of linen and cloth rags.

European paper-making techniques were very similar to those the Chinese had developed more than a thousand years before, although small improvements were gradually introduced. Instead of using grass or horsehair for the mesh of the frames, fine copper wire was soldered together to make a sieve. The wires created a visual effect: after the water has drained through the mesh the fibres tend to lie more thickly in the trough between the strands of wire, leaving an almost "bald" patch on the highest point of the rounded wire. When dried, the paper is more transparent where it is thinnest, and these white stripes which we still sometimes see in paper are called "laid" lines. Advantage was taken of the effect to identify different paper-makers by creating personal symbols in the paper, known as watermarks. The design was soldered in a continuous thread on top of the wire mesh, so that the emblem would be revealed along with the other wire marks when the finished paper was held up to the light.

One of the most important skills in making paper by hand is to achieve a regular integration of the fibres, so as to give the sheet an even tearing strength; and this was done by shaking the watery pulp within the frame as it was scooped from the vat. Machines have never fully been able to simulate this skill, and modern papers will tear much more easily in one direction than the other—particularly cheaper papers such as newsprint.

The tiny fibres, floating in the water as it is spewed out on to the moving belt of wire mesh in a modern paper-making machine, tend naturally to follow the direction of the flow like logs on a river, rather than interlocking equally in all directions. Machine-made papers thus "split" more easily if they are folded in the direction of the fibres, known as the "grain". Grain is an important factor in the manufacture of books, because paper folds (as well as tears) more easily with it than against it. A book bound with the paper grain running horizontally will be less pleasant to handle, because the pages will stand up stiffly rather than lying and folding easily.

Grain direction was not, however, a problem for the early printers. Machine-made paper by the Fourdrinier process did not come into being until the early nineteenth century. They had other problems, nonetheless, since they were often forced to print on paper of uneven thickness and differing weight and size. A newly-formed sheet of moist rag paper in its frame can weigh several pounds, but when dry it weighs only as many ounces. Paper-makers found it hard to judge accurately the rate of evaporation and the potential weight of different pulp constituents, so the manufacture of uniform sheets for printing remained extremely difficult until the onset of the machine age.

However, paper was an immense improvement on its only competitor, parchment, which was much more costly and even more liable to variations in thickness. We have seen that a great printed Bible of Gutenberg's time required as many as three hundred sheepskins for a single volume. The cheapness of paper encouraged easy and ephemeral writing, and it made the printing of books in quantity a practicable possibility for the first time.

The Papermaker by Jost Amman.

8. Copperplate and the Writing Masters

By their adoption of the humanist Roman and Italic scripts as their models for the designs of type, the Italian printers helped to standardise the appearance of the written word throughout almost the whole of Europe. Only in Germany, where printers had designed Gothic typefaces based on the old Gothic script, did another major strand survive from the countless varieties of scripts which spread westwards from the Phoenicians. The printers also drove calligraphy out of the book-production business, leaving it only to influence personal handwriting in the schoolroom, or the commercial scripts of the counting-house and lawyer's office. The handwriting that was taught in schools naturally reflected the major strands which printed books had firmly established as the main styles for written communication. The flurry of publications by Italian writing masters was followed by native manuals elsewhere in Europe: Yciar's *Arte subtilissima* in Spain in 1548; Caspar Neff's introduction of the Italic script into Germany in 1549; and in France Pierre Hamon's *Alphabet de l'invention des lettres en diverses escritures* in 1561. The pure Italian chancery hand was made more popular at court and among scholars in England when Jean de Beauchesne and John Baildon published *A Booke containing divers sortes of hands* in 1570, and the scholar Roger Ascham himself wrote beautifully in the Italian style, and taught it to his royal and aristocratic pupils. The cursive version of the blackletter Gothic script, known as the "running secretary hand", was also widely used in commercial circles and by educated people generally. Indeed it was the handwriting of Shakespeare himself, who poked fun at the new-fangled humanist import by calling it the "sweet Roman hand" (in *Twelfth Night*, written around 1601).

In France, the principal hands of the period, as in England, included a blackletter cursive called *lettres Françoises*, or *lettres financières*, widely used for business purposes, and the aristocratic *Italien Bastarde* for formal correspondence and for diplomatic use. The Low Countries, too, produced excellent examples of copybooks at the hand of Clement Perret, whose *Exercitatio alphabetica* was published in 1569, and Jan van der Velde in his *Spiegel der Schriftkonste* (1605). The writing masters everywhere in Europe promoted their wares with ever more fanciful and decorative figures.

They had been greatly assisted in developing their individual offerings, and in decorating them, by the arrival of a new technical process, copperplate engraving. This could imitate even the finest hairline strokes and flourishes of the schoolmaster-scribe's favourite style without the disadvantages of the relatively crude and fragile wood-block printing method of Arrighi's day. But the pointed burin of the engraver displaced the stronger forms produced by the chisel-edged nib of the pen, and

Sharpening and trimming his students' quill pens must have been an interminable chore for the schoolmaster in the days before the steel pen. Painting by Gerrard Dou, 1671.

introduced and encouraged the meticulous building up of disconnected engraved strokes with a narrow-pointed pen, which was cut specially to respond to the pressure of the writer's hand. Only thus could he imitate the swelling gradation of the swashed and free-swinging forms demanded by the copybook impressions of the engraver's. The *intaglio* printing technique from copper was first developed as a method of reproducing illustrations in the early fifteenth century. It was discovered that even the narrowest of shallow lines engraved or scratched into the polished surface of a flat copper plate retains printing ink in the groove thus formed even after the surface of the copper was skilfully wiped and polished clean. When dampened (and therefore soft) paper was pressed into this groove it picked up the ink and the result was an exceedingly crisp and faithful print of the original line.

The working method used by the metal engraver was already traditional in the gold and silversmiths' trade and indeed the same techniques are still used in the trade today. The engraver's tool or burin is made from a short piece of sharpened steel set into a stubby wooden handle which fits snugly into the palm of the right hand. The burin is held almost stationary and the thick and thin strokes are created by manipulating the downward pressure of the point as it cuts into the copper. The plate is slowly spun, on a rounded leather pad, towards the graver directed by the left hand of the craftsman. He follows a design sketched in reverse on to the plate. The design is transferred by pencil or is lightly scratched with a stylus and can easily be polished off when the engraving is finished. Any "slips" or heavy scratches can be removed by hammering the back of the plate, thus raising the upper surface at the "scene of the crime". The error can then be removed by grinding the surface flat, enabling the engraver to make a fresh start. The intaglio technique is not suitable for printing large letters which have a thick stem, since it is difficult to wipe the surface clean without also removing some of the ink from the bottom of the wide shallow groove. Furthermore, if the engraving is too deep it may hold such a large quantity of ink that it will spread beyond the intended image when a print is taken from it.

After inking the plate and removing most of the surplus ink the printer polishes away the remaining smears by burnishing the plate clean with the palm of his hand which he has first coated in fine chalk, no doubt being careful to remember the words of many a master printer to his apprentice that a good craftsman can be recognised by his dirty hands and clean work whereas a bad craftsman is soon detected by his clean hands and dirty work. A felt blanket is placed between the roller of the press and the dampened paper which is laid on the plate; this helps to force the paper into the ink-filled grooves as the roller passes over it. The result in print can be detected by hand as well as by eye since it is this printing method that produces the slightly raised "feel" which is a characteristic still of certain hand-printed business letter-headings and invitation cards.

The writing masters were quick to seize upon the possibilities this technique offered, and no less quick to advertise the outcome. But their bombastic self-advertisement probably concealed a growing sense of unease and insecurity among the professional practitioners of writing, for although in some respects their market was enlarging with the growth of trade and the expansion of literacy, they were increasingly conscious that these processes had removed their monopoly of the art itself. The professional writing master, who set up in business to teach writing and arithmetic, enjoyed a much humbler position in society than perhaps he felt himself to deserve, as heir to the medieval master-scribes. It was unclear whether he was an artist, a law-writing scrivener or merely a teacher. He no longer enjoyed the status of the priestly scribe in medieval society, nor was he a member of a team of artists and craftsmen who produced sumptuous luxury volumes which were sought after by the highest in the land. The artist-illuminator in the fifteenth and sixteenth centuries had found a new role as an easel-painter, independent of the book, but the calligrapher had lost his association with the making of

The engraver sharpens the point of his lozenge-shaped burin.

beautiful and valuable things. The arrival of the printed book, and the social changes of the following century, forced him into a no-man's-land which to some extent he might be said to occupy still, falling uncomfortably between the stools of scrivener and schoolmaster.

The schoolmaster had always been disliked in the popular mind, and the bully of many a nightmare. In the fourteenth century a master of arts taking his degree was formally presented with a rod of birch which he was expected to use on his pupils, and this fifteenth-century poem still evokes an uneasy response from us today:

> *Brainy teacher, is it your*
> *Desire to beat us daily more,*
> *Like a blooming Lord?*
> *We'd rather leave your school for good,*
> *And learn another livelihood*
> *Than jump to your bossy word.*

How pleased that poet would have been to hear about another English schoolmaster who was recorded as having drowned in a mill pond in 1301 while climbing a willow tree to replenish his stock of canes!

The "mere scrivener" too was widely vilified, particularly in the seventeenth and eighteenth centuries in England, when the trade had become associated in the public mind with money-lending and the cunning and sometimes unscrupulous writing of legal contracts and other documents. To the illiterate public the scrivener was a fraud and twister, an artful

A copperplate printer's workshop in the mid-17th century. In the background one man forces ink into the engraved plate. At the left another man cleans off the ink from the surface, polishing it with the palm of his hand; while a printer on his right turns the steel roller which forces the damp paper into the ink-filled design.

purveyor of legal jargon designed to mystify the plain man. A scurrilous pamphlet published in Oxford in 1667 gives some indication why the writing master resented being placed in such company, and felt the need so stridently to protest his worth and education.

> *A London scrivener is a creature begot by a pen, and hatcht up in an inkpot . . . the wing of a goose sets up forty of them. His gown . . . has as little wool upon it, as if at next remove it were to be made Parchment;—The Attorney may have the honour to go to Hell on horseback, while the base Knave fairly foots it after him. . . . Where they once get in, they spread like the itch and become as universal as the Sickness; had a Scrivener bin among the Israelites, there needed no other punishment to have forced them out of Egypt: They themselves had bin the greatest plague, and Pharaoh would have fled, not pursued them.*

Even in his role alongside the moneylender his position was distinctly inferior, as the pamphlet goes on:

> *[After they have tricked a young heir into their clutches], like the Lyon and the Jackall they divide the prey; the Usurer gnaws off all the flesh, and the Scrivener picks the bone.*

And if by this time we are left in any doubt about the views of this particular author on the subject of scriveners, the tirade ends:

> *may he be poyson'd with his own Ink, stab'd with his Penknife . . . his nodle [head] set out at the Shop-door for a Loggerhead, and the rest of him hang'd up to Eternity in a Label; and since it is impossible he should get into heaven, for Hell's sake may he hang between.*

The copybooks and writing exemplars tended to be sprinkled with Latin texts and extracts from the classics, and great pains were taken to procure a preface or foreword from a distinguished patron to give respectability to a new publication. When the calligraphers were not fighting for recognition, moreover, they were fighting each other. In 1595 two English calligraphers, Peter Bailes and Daniel Johnson, took part in a trial of penmanship, competing for a prize of "a golden pen of twentie pounds". Johnson, a bad loser, afterwards published a manifesto protesting that the jury had been rigged, and Bailes counter-charged with a denunciation of his own. Many of the great eighteenth-century masters, Shelley, Snell, John Clark, Snow and Ollyffe, for example, continued to denounce one another in prefaces or in the public prints. It was a sad spectacle, for whatever their public antics the skills of these masters and of their engravers were without doubt immense. The Renaissance scribes of Italy had never needed to compete with a machine, or with the razzle-dazzle of the engraver's slick allure which placed a barrier between the pen and the page. The chain was broken, and the writing master postured on the stage of a sideshow, teaching children, producing elaborate citations and squabbling with his rivals, while the other arts drew still further away from him.

Notaries' marks, appended to the documents they authenticated. *Opposite. Two Tax Gatherers* by Quentin Massys (1464–1530).

The title page of Edward
Cocker's *The Pen's Tran-
scendencie* (1657).

Although the designs for the copperplate were originally sketched out
by pen on paper or parchment by the writing master, it is important to
bear in mind that, since the exemplars are not written but engraved from
a tracing of the written original, they have a deliberate perfection
derived from the slow process of the engraver's skill. The very word
"engraved" has a slow unwinding sound to it. A pen is an immediate and
spontaneous mark-making instrument, which can capture the slightest
tremor of the moving hand, directed by the mind and eye. The marks
require speed to give them life. As much of the calligraphic art of the
East well testifies, handwritten words can thus be elevated to the highest
form of abstract expression.

But the engraver's burin must move more slowly and slightly. The
plate alone moves and spins on its polished leather pad, the copper
steadily pushed towards the biting point of the steel tool in the strong
hands of the engraver. The result is a hollow counterfeit of the pen's
life-like strokes. The slowly and laboriously made letters have a wiry
perfection which mocks the student who tries to emulate its second-
hand finery and brilliant tricks.

Under all the flourishes, however, lies a very simple, useful and
practicable cursive hand which allows the writer to produce word after
word without lifting the pen between letters. Like the Carolingian
minuscule it would not have survived so long and so successfully if it had
not been useful and practical, and in its own way handsome. But the
truth is that its range of visual textures is limited. The simple push-pull,
up-thin and down-thick swelling of the pen under pressure does not
provide enough diversion to hold the eye's interest for long. Its beauty is
skin deep, like a pretty boy or girl with an empty head. The writing
masters' hard-sell of this simple script, decking it out in more and more
finery, making the most extravagant claims for their work and confusing

art with showmanship, merely compounded the arguments of their detractors, who claimed that calligraphy, if it meant penmanship, could never be art.

Once we appreciate the causes of the artistic limbo which the writing masters occupied, their claims and posturings provide not only amusement but some insight into the nature of society in their day.

Not every writing master defended extravagant flourishes and decoration, although almost all indulged in them nonetheless. Martin Billingsley, writing master to Charles I, wrote around 1616 that:

> to use any strange, borrowed or inforc'd tricks and knots in or about writing other then with the celerity of the hand are to be performed, is rather to set an inglorious glosse upon a simple peece of worke, than to give a comely lustre to a perfect patterne; they being as unnaturall to writing as a surfet is to a temperate man's body.

Edward Cocker (1631–76) on the other hand, the outstanding and aptly-named showman-scribe of his time, did not agree and put his cards firmly on the table:

> Some sordid sotts
> Cry downe rare knotts,
> But art shall shine
> And envie pine
> And still my pen shall flourish.

Cocker would have rejected our sympathy for the precarious position of the writing master in society, and held an unquestioning faith in his own ability and in the grandeur of his profession. On the title page of his first book he proclaimed (with more confidence than poetic skill):

THE PEN'S TRANSCENDENCIE

or

FAIRE WRITING'S LABYRINTH

Wherein Faire Writing to the Life's exprest
In sundry Copies, cloth'd with Art's rich Vest
By wch. with practice, thou may'st gaine Perfection,
As th'Heav'n-taught Author did, without direction.

Invented, Written and Engraved by
EDWARD COCKER

One is reminded irresistibly of Eadwine "the prince of writers": "The excellence of my work proclaims my worthiness."

The same arguments raged on in the small world of the writing masters through the seventeenth century and beyond, and the rival protagonists fell broadly into two opposing schools. There was the no-nonsense attitude of those like Charles Snell (1667–1733), who condemned the inclusion of "owls, apes and monsters and sprigg'd letters" in a book on writing. On the other hand his opponents felt equally strongly, in the words of John Clark (1683–1736), that whilst "plain, easy and useful examples in several hands" might fit students for the world of business, "the practice of striking and sprigging letters are pretty ingenious exercises for use at their leisure hours, and may also serve to please such as may admire the fancy of the pen as well as the solid use of it". No doubt he and those who felt like him were still voicing, at heart, a nostalgia for the great days of the illuminated book that had now gone forever.

One of the most important figures in the middle of the eighteenth century, whose influence continued long after its close, was George Bickham. In his splendid book *The Universal Penman*, published in parts between 1733 and 1741, he proclaimed the view that writing was "The first step and the essential in setting up a man of business . . . Plain, strong and neat writing as it best answers the designs for use and beauty; so it has most obtained among men of business". This was the case for the minuscule hand of the copperplate script, expressed in its simplest form. It was indeed eminently useful for a burgeoning class of people who needed to write quickly and legibly in the course of their work. Yet, having stated this simple proposition, Bickham proceeded to decorate many of his two hundred and twelve folio plates with elaborate pictorial engravings of his alphabet at work—"The whole embellish'd with beautiful decorations for the amusement of the curious".

Isaac D'Israeli, father of the British prime minister, viewed the antics of the writing masters with disdain. "Never," he wrote, "has there been a race of professors in any art who have exceeded in solemnity and pretention the practitioners in this simple and mechanical craft . . . a pen in one hand, and a trumpet in the other."

But when all is said and done there can be no denying that the be-wigged eighteenth-century dandies who strut in their finery among the illustrations and vignettes in Bickham's writing books do not reflect the spirit of their age any more accurately than do the curlicues and engraved scripts which accompany them. Once again letters, like men, "resemble their age more than they do their fathers".

Elsewhere, the German running hand, heir to the Gothic book script, continued to occupy a peculiar position in Europe. The cursive version of Gothic which had developed alongside the Italian chancery script had been superseded in England and France by copperplate, and survived there only in its use in the legal profession. In German-speaking countries, however, the running hand remained for four centuries the only correspondence script in general use, surviving until the 1940s. In France, as we have seen, copperplate-engraved exemplars in the *bastarde* style—a compromise between the italic shapes made by a square-cut pen and the hairline joins of the burin—gained wide circulation in the early seventeenth century, and indeed played a major part in spreading such styles to Britain. Perhaps unfairly, the forms of copperplate hand which developed from it returned to Europe under the name of *lettres anglaises*, and were reproduced in type specimen books in France and Germany (where in printed form they were called the

Precept and practice. The perfumier's elegantly hand-engraved notepaper puts the readable but much less accomplished efforts of Mr Bassett to shame. A blunt quill pen was no match for the product of the engraver.

English running hand).

Calligraphy had now become handwriting embellished for those who "may admire the fancy of the pen as well as the solid use of it", in John Clark's words. The student laboured, tongue in teeth, as he painstakingly copied the engraved texts and struggled to control the pointed quill tip. They exhorted him in firm moral tones to "avoid bad company, confine your passion, and endeavour to improve".

But the many different styles developed in the copybooks—from plain

book scripts to elaborately flourished cursive hands, elegantly reconstructed classical capitals and letters made up of grotesquely writhing Gothic strapwork—were put to more uses than the teaching of handwriting. They were widely used as pattern-books by many different craftsmen—jewellers, goldsmiths and embroiderers as well as carvers in wood, brass and stone. In the seventeenth and eighteenth centuries these styles can often be clearly connected with their copybook sources. During the classical revival in art and architecture in England the inscriptional letters of the Italian Renaissance again came into vogue, and for the first time since the Romans had departed nearly fifteen hundred years before the stately *capitalis monumentalis* graced the walls and porticos of Bath and York once more.

Writing masters could seldom resist sugaring the pill with miscellaneous examples of their virtuosity.

9. Writing in a Machine Age

Although the quill had been an enormously successful writing instrument for many centuries after it superseded the reed pen in the early days of Christianity in the West, its supremacy had not always been unchallenged. The Romans, we know, made pens out of various metals; and even in the Middle Ages, when Gutenberg's former partners printed their first book, they felt it necessary to state in the colophon that:

> this work is fashioned and by diligence finished for the service of God, not with ink of quill nor brazen reed but with a certain invention of printing and reproducing by John Fust, citizen of Maintz, and Peter Schoeffer of Gernsheim, 17 December 1465 AD.

Over the centuries individual inventors and manufacturers in different countries had attempted to make some form or other of metal substitute for the quill. In 1700 Roger North wrote to his sister:

> You will hardly tell by what you see that I write with a steel pen. It is a device come out of France. . . . When they get the knack of making them exactly, I do not doubt but the government of the goose quill is near an end, for none that can have them will use other.

It is hardly surprising that strenuous efforts should have been made to overthrow the "government of the goose quill", for although in professional hands it was an expressive and fluent writing instrument, like a modern racing car it needed constant skilled and fine adjustment to ensure continuous high performance. By the mid-eighteenth century there was an increasing demand for a simple and durable pen for business and school use.

As often happens, invention quickly followed upon the heels of necessity in several places simultaneously, and there were a number of claims to the title of "first inventor" of metal pens. A manuscript book of 1748 placed on record the claim of Johann Jantssen, a magistrate of Aix-la-Chapelle (Aachen), who felt that he might "without boasting, claim the honour of having invented a new pen. It is perhaps no accident that God should have inspired me at the present time with the idea of making steel pens." (He had just managed to sell his entire stock to visiting members of a diplomatic congress.) "They are now sent into every corner of the world as a rare thing—to Spain, France, England, and Holland. Others will no doubt make imitations of my pens, but I am the man who first invented and made them."

The *Boston Mechanic* in August 1835, however, published a note that the inventor of steel pens (in 1800) was an American, "a well-known resident of our city, Mr Peregrine Williamson . . . The English soon borrowed the invention, [and] realised immense fortunes." A German

publication gave the credit to a schoolteacher of Königsberg, who in 1808 made pens from metal "but got poor by his efforts". A pamphlet on the manufacture of steel pens published in Paris in 1884 naturally attributed the invention to a Frenchman, who made metal pens in the 1750s as a curiosity; but "this invention did not have any immediate result in France, but spread to England, and became in Birmingham about 1830 a very prosperous industry".

Craftsmen in England, too, had experimented with various metals, including brass and steel, for recreating the qualities of the quill; and also with such materials as horn and tortoiseshell embedded with tiny pieces of precious stone and reinforced by thin strips of gold. Nibs made entirely from gold were flexible and pleasant to use, but they were expensive and soon wore out. In due course methods were invented for working with thin strip steel, and it replaced other materials for general use. At first each pen was produced laboriously and sometimes crudely by hand. The most difficult process in the early days was to make the right kind of slit in the pen. One way was to hammer a thin strip of metal into a tube shape, so that as the outer edges drew together they created the slit. The underside of the tube was then scooped away just like a quill, and the end filed into shape. Another technique, similar in principle to later machine-methods, involved roughly punching the shape of the pen out of a flat sheet of soft steel, and then rounding this

Kit's Writing Lesson by R. B. Martineau (1826–69).

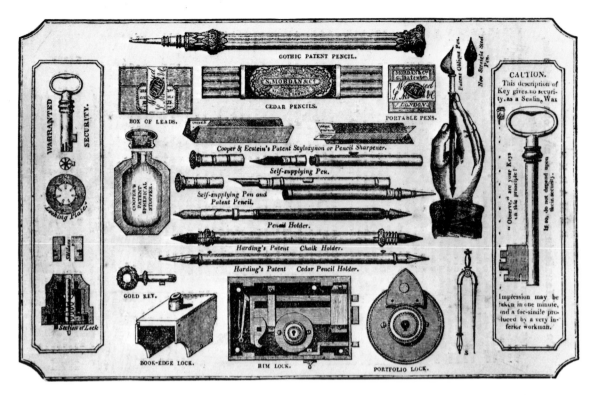

GOTHIC PATENT PENCIL.

CEDAR PENCILS.

BOX OF LEADS.

PORTABLE PENS.

WARRANTED SECURITY.

Locking Plate.

Slides

Section of Lock

Cooper & Ecstein's Patent Stylozynon or Pencil Sharpener.

Self-supplying Pen.

Self-supplying Pen and Patent Pencil.

Pencil Holder.

Harding's Patent Chalk Holder.

Harding's Patent Cedar Pencil Holder.

GOLD KEY.

BOOK-EDGE LOCK.

RIM LOCK.

PORTFOLIO LOCK.

Patent Oblique Pen.

New Straight Steel Pen.

CAUTION. This description of Key gives no security, as a Sealing Wax

"Observe," are your Keys on this principle?

If so, do not depend upon their security.

Impression may be taken in one minute, and a fac-simile produced by a very inferior workman.

In the early days each pen point was manufactured individually by hand. Among the locks and gadgets advertised here is an early attempt at a "self-supplying" pen.

"blank" into a nib shape by hammering it over a circular rod of wood or lead. The underside of the point was then marked by a sharp chisel into the steel where the slit was to be made, and when the steel was hardened this dent could be forced to crack along its length. Finally, the end was ground and shaped by a file or wheel to create the required nibpoint. It was soon apparent, however, that a single slit in steel, exactly copying the quill, was not enough to give the right amount of flexibility, either to allow a steady flow of ink to the pen point, or to impart the right feel which users of the goose quill would have felt natural. So two more short slits were made on either side of the main one. The early tube pens were slipped over wooden holders or an uncut quill which fitted comfortably in the hand. Others were equipped with screws which twisted into a metal handle.

The manufacturers of these handmade "cracked slit" pens laid the basis of the early pen industry in Birmingham, which helped that English Midlands town to become "the workshop of the world", breathlessly adulated by nineteenth-century British gazetteers for its arts and industry: "Distinguished for a spirit of enterprise united with habits of perserverance: for a rare association of genius to invent, and hands to execute, altogether unparalleled in the annals of commerce." Other cities elsewhere in the world were also wakening to the industrial dawn; but at least as far as pens were concerned the manufacturers of Birmingham had indeed recognised a saleable idea when they saw it, and so set about producing metal pen nibs in quantity for markets at home and abroad.

Handmade steel pens, of course, were very expensive. Nor did everyone welcome the change, since the early pens were stiff and rigid, and the unpliant metal dug easily into the surface of the paper. The quill-maker also fought back by producing ready-made "pen nibs" cut from quills, which not only catered for the traditionalists but could also be used in the fancy new "pen sticks" or holders which were undoubtedly attracting customers to the new-fangled steel pens of their competitors.

But time was running against such rearguard actions, and in 1830 Mr James Perry was able to announce that "till about 6 months ago the public had heard little of metallic pens. At present, it would seem that comparatively few of any *other* kind are in the hands of any class of the community. This sudden transition may clearly be traced to the announcement of the Patent Perryian Pens in various periodicals about 6 months ago."

This super-salesman made use of a new aspect of the spread of literacy: the printing press and the spread of education had created a large mass of people susceptible for the first time to advertising on a grand scale. Through the medium of newspapers and journals Perry lectured them on the virtues of his improved, Patent, Birmingham-made pens; and linked this to his Perryian system of education. Other practical factors also helped him. The smooth surface of cheaply produced machine-made paper by the Fourdrinier method, which was available in the 1820s, was much more compatible with the sharp point of the steel pen than the rough hand-made paper of the quill pen era. And when more benign alternatives were found to the acid-based inks which had quickly corroded the first steel pens, another objection was removed.

There was also the question of writing styles. The engraved copperplate scripts of the writing masters had continued in vogue throughout the eighteenth and early nineteenth centuries, and they placed impossible demands on the flimsy quill pen and on the skills of its users. To copy the style produced by the engraving tool a very fine and fragile point was needed, and maintaining such a point on a quill was a laborious and tricky process. Even Sir Rowland Hill, the "father of the postal system", who did so much to spread the uses of literacy, made such a poor job of trimming quills that in the days before the mass-produced steel pen, when he taught schoolchildren to write, he had to seek the help of his brother to mend the pens which had been butchered by the children the week before. The poet Thomas Hood sums up the gratitude that thousands of people in the mid-nineteenth century must have felt for the simplicities of the new pens:

In times begone, when each man cut his quill
With little Perryian *skill;*
What horrid, awkward, bungling tools of trade
Appeared the writing instruments, home made!
What pens were sliced, hewed, hacked, and haggled out,
Slit or unslit, with many a various snout,
Aquiline, Roman, crooked, square, and snubby,
Humpy and stubby . . .
To try in any common inkstands then,

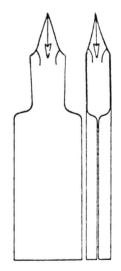

The cracked-slit barrel pen made from flat steel before rounding.

133

With all their miscellaneous stocks,
To find a decent pen,
Was like a dip into a lucky box;
You drew, and got one very curly,
And split like endive in some hurly-burly;
The next unslit, a square at end, a spade;
The third, incipient pop-gun, not yet made;
The fourth a broom; the fifth of no avail,
Turned upwards, like a rabbit's tail;
And last, not least, by way of a relief,
A stump that Master Richard, James, or John
Had tried his candle cookery upon,
Making "roast beef"!

Stray references to the problems of pen-making ("Excuse haste and bad pen, as the pig said as he ran up the street") are common in nineteenth-century literature, and one can see why people were willing to pay high prices for those first hand-made steel pens.

The time was ripe, the technology was available, and the ground had been prepared by advertising like that of James Perry, for the mass-production of pens by machine. When a craftsman set up shop in a back-street warren in early nineteenth-century Birmingham, he rented not only the premises but steam power. This is how Joseph and William Gillott started making small pen-knives in a "badly lit unsanitary manufactory" in the 1820s. Surplus power from a neighbour's engine was used to operate machinery in other workshops clustered nearby. The button-makers, bottle-jack manufacturers, needle and pin factories and iron founders came up with the answers that had eluded the pen-makers of the past. Wholesalers, like Perry, had their stocks provided by small workshops which had already produced them in large quantities by hand processes. But within thirty years from 1820 the application of machinery for stamping and slitting pens had reduced their price from 2d each to 2d per gross—and this even included the box. The names of the early workshops who sold to wholesalers like Perry remained obscure; but mass-produced pens, made in countless shapes and sizes by machine, turned companies like Gillott and Mitchell into household names all over the world.

The essential breakthrough was the application to pen-making of the screw-press used in button manufacture and other trades. This machine was capable of stamping out accurate shapes from thin sheets of metal and other materials, and could also be adapted for the rounding and splitting of nibs. Sheets of soft steel rolled to a uniform thickness were cut into ribbons, and fed into a fly press by a skilled operator who stamped out as many as 28,000 pen blanks in a single day. Each stamp was accurately placed close to its neighbour so as to waste as little sheet steel as possible. The blanks were then "marked", stamped with the maker's name or trade mark, and any other information required. Hundreds of hotels in America, for example, from New York to the "wild west", were supplied with pens thus marked with the name of the

METALLIC

Pen Maker

TO THE

QUEEN

Opposite. Using machine production techniques, some of the small pen manufacturers in the back streets of Birmingham became household names all over the world.

134

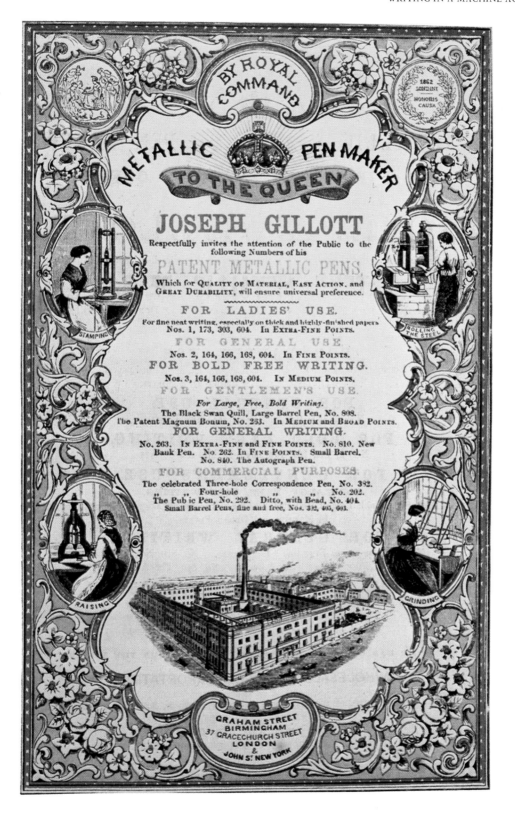

Scrap   Cutting

Marking   Piercing

Embossing   Raising

Grinding   Slitting

establishment for the exclusive use of their patrons.

The next step was to pierce the blank with side slits to give the pen extra flexibility, and further resilience could be added at the same time by piercing holes through the metal, particularly in the centre where the main slits terminated. In order to emboss a raised design on to the blank, and to press it into the rounded shape needed for the pen, the steel must be soft and pliable. The accurate punches and dies which interlock and press the flat steel into a perfect image of themselves were the product of great skill on the part of the toolmakers.

Once formed into the shape of pen nibs, the thousands of soft steel pieces were hardened, and their points further thinned by grinding, to prepare them for splitting. Here another screw press was employed, with an upper and lower cutter. Fed individually between metal guides, the shaped pen-points were exactly centred between the cutters, which made the final clean split in the centre of the nib. Any roughness left by the tooling on the edges of the nibs was finally removed by "tumbling" them for several hours in barrels with fine abrasives such as walnut shells; and finally they were polished in the same way by sawdust. "Colour" was imparted by heating them in cylinders over a coke fire until the requisite tint, achieved by varying temperatures, was reached. The pens were then lacquered, to prevent rusting, and dried.

By the end of the nineteenth century the thirteen principal pen factories in Birmingham were between them using some 28 tons of the finest thin steel per week, and producing from it some 175 million pen nibs every year. These were boxed and despatched to markets in every part of the world. In less than fifty years the quill pen was banished into obscurity. This remarkable story of growth, and the dominance of the Birmingham-based making of pens, was achieved by the improvement of manufacturing methods; but it should not be forgotten that sweated labour played its part. The young women who gladly worked through the night in the Birmingham factories not only received pitiful wages, but also had to bring their own candles to light them at their work. They thus made it possible for the steel pen to become one of the first "throw-away" commodities to be produced in the industrial era.

Ink

The inks which had served clerks and scribes so well for centuries did not suit the new steel pens. The brown ink which we can still see in countless manuscripts written with a quill produced a powerful chemical reaction with steel, and quickly rusted the fine pen point away. These inks were chiefly made from a mixture of oak galls and iron salts, and they were highly practical and successful for their original purpose. An alternative, which had also been used by professional scribes from earliest times, was the more permanent carbon ink, similar to Egyptian writing fluid dating back as far as 2500 BC. This was made from soot, water and gum. It had no adverse chemical effect on steel, but it tended to clog the pen, and did not always store well in bottles.

Advances in the science of chemistry, and the improved availability of

This well-lit Birmingham pen nib factory around the turn of the century was probably untypical.

dyes, allowed alternatives to be developed. One of the first ink factories was set up in 1834 to cater for the new demand, and its proprietors, Messrs Stephens, advertised their new patent writing fluids in strident terms in Robson's *London Directory* for 1834: "... will accomplish the so long desired and apparently hopeless task of rendering the manuscript as durable and indelible as the printed record. It is proof against every known chemical agent, and combines with the paper and parchment so strongly as to resist moisture and every other influence." This ink no doubt contained some carbon, since it is called "carbonaceous black writing fluid"; but the "Dark Blue", "Light Blue" and "Brilliant Red ... more strikingly beautiful and durable than any Red solution hitherto used" were probably chemically based.

James Perry, naturally, was not far behind. His advertisement in the *Polytechnic Review* of 1843 announced:

PERRYIAN LYMPID INK

This ink has a flowing property peculiar to itself, and does not corrode metallic pens as other inks.

This was offered both in bottles and in powder form. In 1856, aniline dyes were discovered and soon provided another advance in the search for non-corrosive inks which would run freely without soaking or spreading into the paper, and which did not smell or go bad.

The non-specialist inks which we buy in bottles today bear little relationship to the formulae of these early efforts, since they are designed for use in fountain pens which have different needs. But they survived as late as the 1940s, when in powdered form they were widely used in schools. By the 1850s, indeed, ink, pen and paper had reached a level of technical efficiency from which there was little major advance until the arrival of the ballpoint pen. Even as early as 1838 Henry Stephen was advertising "newly-formed fountain holders"; and the *Penny Cyclopaedia* published in 1840 defined fountain pen as "a pen made with a reservoir in its stem or holder, to supply ink for some time without replenishing . . ." During this long period, instead of looking for major technical advances the penmakers concentrated upon marketing. The variety of pen-sticks or holders which were designed and sold from the 1840s on almost defies description. Elaborate silver and bejewelled holders, ebony, gold and glass in marvellous profusion, adorned the stationers' shop-windows and seaside souvenir stalls. Even the mid-nineteenth-century electro-therapeutic craze was grist to the pen-makers' mill: they came out with "electric pens" which were claimed to be good for "calming nervous fingers"!

Nibs too were created in thousands of different shapes and sizes, one factory producing as many as four hundred different patterns at the same time. There were commemorative pens, portrait pens, patent Axissary pens, regulating pens, and special nibs for the writing of Arabic scripts. A clever invention was the so-called "elbow-pen", designed to overcome the awkwardness experienced by right-handed people writing in the exaggerated forward-sloping hand demanded by some of the copperplate cursive scripts. In this respect the quill pen, with its curve to the right, had a natural advantage over the straight pen nib, and the elbow-pen was designed to emulate it.

All these ingenious devices were peddled by the nineteenth-century salesmen, some of whose companies sold their Birmingham-made pens through subsidiaries set up in Germany and France to imply a local origin for the goods. The elaborately designed and printed boxes were tailored for many national markets abroad, such as the Railway and Goorkha pens for India, the Danskpost pen for Denmark, and the Admiral Tojo pen for Japan.

They were not, of course, without competitors and rivals. By the 1890s there were some half a dozen well-established pen factories in Europe, and at least two in the United States. Enthusiasm for the wonders of technology and science, and their exploitation by factory methods, was a world-wide phenomenon; and the great Expositions in France, the trade fairs in Germany and even the beginnings of industrialisation in the most backward of all European countries, Russia, testified to an almost universal faith in the bright new world founded on the success of the machine.

On the other hand, there were those who questioned this faith and pointed to some of the negative effects of the "wonders of the age". The art critic John Ruskin, for example, was among the first in the 1850s to criticise not only the shapes of some of the products of machines, but the

The Birmingham-based pen industry penetrated markets all over the world. They sold their nibs in sumptuously produced boxes, some of whose labels had foreign addresses but were printed in Birmingham.

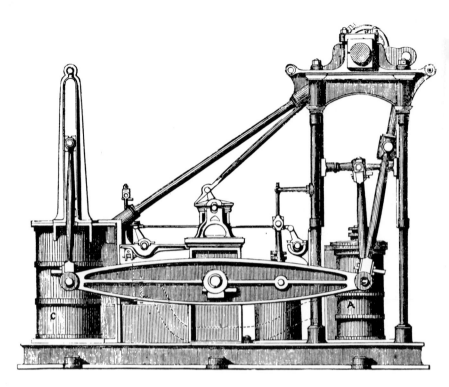

The machines themselves often possessed more grace and simplicity than the fussy products they were designed to make, like this bird-table/flower-stand.

morality of a system which forced men and women to produce objects over whose design they had no control. Before the Industrial Revolution there had often been a close relationship between the maker and the buyer. We have seen how in the production of books this general rule applied: how the Dean and Chapter of York commissioned their service books with a precise awareness of the techniques to be employed, and how even when a scribe was responsible for only part of an illuminated book, the chain between himself and the customer was short enough to have real meaning for him. The machinists making pen nibs, however, and even the owner of the factory in which they worked, were by no means always the people who sold them in the market place. Mr Perry was neither a craftsman nor a manufacturer: he was a successful distributor and salesman. The pen which worked best in his eyes was one which performed well on a balance sheet. The machine became the supreme craftsman, and unchecked by the traditional limitations placed on the design of articles made singly by the human hand, the machine's products often showed an absurd and unbalanced lack of restraint. Kenneth Clark (in his book *Civilisation*) has expressed his doubts that works of art exhibited at the Great Exhibition at the Crystal Palace in 1851 could ever come back into favour, because they do not express any real conviction. The building in which they were housed, however, did possess a simple and strong authority because it was designed by an engineer (Joseph Paxton) who certainly saw it as a kind of machine. It was the machine itself which received the best efforts of the best nineteenth-century inventors and designers. Its products were for the most part by-products, incidental to their main creative concern. No wonder these

The pen industry gained greatly from the rise of advertising, which became almost an art form in its own right.

manufactures lacked conviction.

It was hardly surprising that observers like Ruskin and his followers should be intensely aware of the lack, in both spirit and image, of the new industrial products. For one thing the handmade craftsmanship of the last half-century was still present everywhere, to mock the poverty of its machine-made shadows. The reaction, inevitably, took the form of a desire to return to pre-industrial values; but the cry for the "honest craftsmanship" of the past was so successful in reaching an audience already prepared to some extent by the Gothic revival in architecture and art that, ironically, it only furthered the public appetite for quaint neo-medievalism. This market was enthusiastically welcomed by the manufacturers, who simply retooled their machines and proceeded to sell even more sham products in quaint new styles with a medieval flavour. It was an illusion to suppose that the processes of industrial-isation and mass-marketing could be reversed by these attempts to "educate" public taste.

It is also Kenneth Clark's view that one can tell more about the nature of past civilisations from their architecture than from anything else they leave behind: architecture "is to some extent a communal art—at least it depends upon a relationship between the user and the maker much closer than in other arts". Much the same may be true of the writing and formal letter forms of any period. The nineteenth-century pursuit of wealth through industrialisation, and the contemporary view of progress which went along with it, fused with the counter-currents of reaction, and can be seen vividly reflected in the alphabets of the nineteenth century. Ornamental penmanship was still very much in existence, for both profit and pleasure. But in this age of self-improvement and the expansion of popular education, the new growth industry was "practical penmanship", encouraged and recommended by men of business. In the U.S.A. in the first half of the century well over 100 writing masters were teaching and publishing writing "systems", many of them based on analytical methods. Their aim was unashamedly to teach rapid writing for the man of business. Foremost among them was Benjamin Franklin Foster, who could boast that in the 1830s some two million of his copybooks had been sold, in America, England and France. Although his system was based on that of the Englishman Carstairs, the French correctly christened it the *système Americaine* in 1828; and indeed almost all of the new analytical systems, including Carstairs', seemed to have stemmed from the publication of John Jenkins' *Art of Writing* in Boston, Massachusetts, in 1791. Like many of the seventeenth-century teachers' manuals on writing and "arithmetick", these systems were often allied to general educational programmes covering most of the normal school syllabus, with familiar titles like "Double-entry elucidated", and "The counting-house assistant". One was sold so successfully that what the English call "copperplate writing" is still known in America as "Spencerian", after its proponent, Platt Rogers Spencer (1800–64). The "push-pull" exercises of yet another system, the Palmer Method, are still remembered with terror by those who were taught by his methods well into the present century.

Just as the mail order catalogues spread across America in the 1860s, bringing the new industrial manufactures to a widely scattered population, so, too, did a host of "self-instructors", including books on penmanship. The sheer weight of superlatives which some of them contained, each climbing on the head of the next in an attempt to be heard, was well within the tradition of writing manuals established for over 300 years. A typical example, from the Royal Publishing Company

Some wholesalers stocked as many as 400 different patterns of pen nibs to cater for the whims of the public.

of Detroit, Michigan, in the early 1890s, is worth quoting from if only because the kind of script it advocated is still the most widely used for personal handwriting throughout America today. The *Real Penwork Instructor in Penmanship* claimed to be "the greatest means ever known for learning to write an elegant hand. Nothing like it ever published before". For one dollar, the publishers maintained:

> *no other publishers in the world are giving the people as much for the money. The largest and most elegantly Illustrated Work on the subject of penmanship ever published in the world. [It] contains more Copies, more Ornamental Work, and more and better Instructions, for learning the Whole Art of Penmanship without a teacher, than any other work published in the World.... When we first perfected the photo-electrographing process for reproducing real pen-work, we realised we had found a means of publishing the greatest book on penmanship ever conceived of.... The whole book so thoroughly explains that you cannot help understanding all about it.*

All this self-recommendation might well arouse our suspicions, but in fact the book does provide, with excellent illustration, a relatively straightforward and clear method for acquiring a visual grasp of the "copperplate-type" alphabet. Each letter is indeed "taken all to pieces, one at a time, and thoroughly analysed and explained by itself, in a plain and simple way". What it does not explain, however, is that like all acquired skills, to do it well is neither easy nor quick, which is what many of these books at least by implication dishonestly claimed. A great deal of perserverance and self-discipline was needed to master the elegant and sometimes eccentric form of a copperplate style.

After fifteen pages of fairly measured common sense, with examples of a practical and useful hand, the *Real Penwork* self-instructor gets down to the real business of the day—sixty-one pages of extravagant flourishes and pictures provided by the "Department of Ornamental Penmanship", including a before and after example provided by Mr

Frank Bliss, twelve years of age, who used their patent tracing process (best quality tracing paper could be obtained from the publishers, six sheets for 25 cents post paid). The section also includes specimens from several eminent penmen of the day, including D. T. Ames, editor of the *Penman's Art Journal*. The reader is invited to "look this department through and you will see a greater variety and more designs of beautiful flourishing and ornamental penwork, than can be found in any other collection in the world . . . it contains specimens of ornamental penwork by nearly all the best penmen who have ever lived and also contains all the masterpieces and best designs and gems of ornamental penmanship executed by W. H. Lyons, the most wonderful penman and genius in art that ever existed." Beat that, Edward Cocker!

As the century drew to a close only the law writers or scriveners remained as professional calligraphers in the historical sense. Their status was reduced and their standards were debased; but they were nonetheless the only genuine surviving professional writers of documents by hand. They received a training of sorts, and many of them still plied their daily trade with a quill pen. In Britain particularly there was a

In *The Real Penwork Instructor* only 15 pages were devoted to writing itself. The remaining 61 pages were covered with flourished decorations.

All the Small Letters Thoroughly Analyzed and Explained.

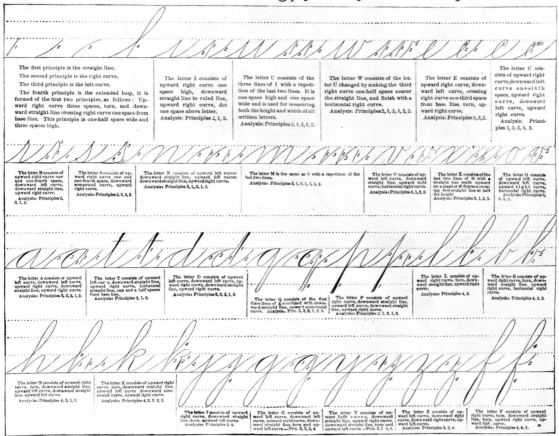

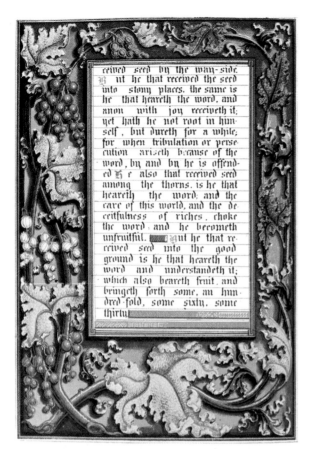

ceived seed by the way-side.
But he that received the seed
into stony places, the same is
he that heareth the word, and
anon with joy receiveth it;
yet hath he not root in himself, but dureth for a while;
for when tribulation or perse-
cution ariseth because of the
word, by and by he is offend-
ed He also that received seed
among the thorns, is he that
heareth the word; and the
care of this world, and the de-
ceitfulness of riches, choke
the word, and he becometh
unfruitful. But he that received seed into the good
ground is he that heareth the
word and understandeth it;
which also beareth fruit, and
bringeth forth some, an hun-
dred-fold, some sixty, some
thirty.

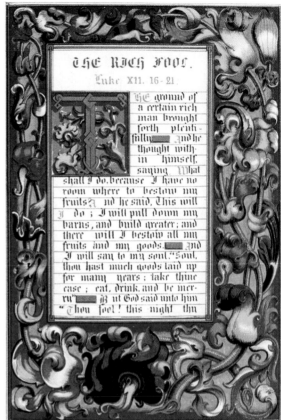

THE RICH FOOL.
Luke XII. 16-21.

The ground of a certain rich man brought forth plenti-fully. And he thought with-in himself, saying, What shall I do, because I have no room where to bestow my fruits? And he said, This will I do; I will pull down my barns, and build greater; and there will I bestow all my fruits and my goods. And I will say to my soul, "Soul, thou hast much goods laid up for many years; take thine ease; eat, drink, and be mer-ry." But God said unto him "Thou fool! this night thy

Mary and her sister Martha.
It was that Mary, which a-
nointed the Lord with ointment,
and wiped his feet with her hair,
whose brother Lazarus was
sick. Therefore his sisters
sent unto him, saying, Lord,
behold he whom thou lovest is
sick. When Jesus heard that,
he said, This sickness is not
unto death, but for the glory of
God, that the son of God might
be glorified thereby. Now
Jesus loved Martha, and her
sister, and Lazarus. When
he had heard, therefore, that
he was sick, he abode two days
still in the same place, where
he was. Then after that saith
he to his disciples, Let us go
into Judea again. His disciples say unto him, Master, the
Jews of late sought to stone

thee; and goest thou thither a-
gain? Jesus answered,
Are there not twelve hours in
the day? If any man walk in
the day, he stumbleth not, because he seeth the light of this
world. But if a man walk in
the night, he stumbleth, because there is no light in him.
These things said he: and after
that he saith unto them, Our
friend Lazarus sleepeth; but
I go that I may awake him out
of sleep. Then said his
disciples, Lord, if he sleep he
shall do well. Howbeit, Jesus
spake of his death; but they
thought he had spoken of taking of rest in sleep. Then said
Jesus unto them plainly, Lazarus is dead. And I am glad
for your sakes that I was not
there, to the intent ye may be-

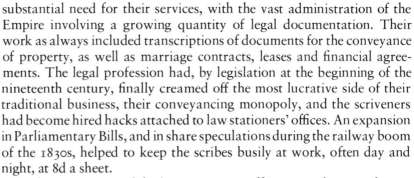

The illustrator Noel Humphreys thought of himself as an illuminator, although he worked with the new medium of chromolithography. These printed illuminated gift books were the first using full colour to reach the public since the hand-produced volumes of the Middle Ages.

substantial need for their services, with the vast administration of the Empire involving a growing quantity of legal documentation. Their work as always included transcriptions of documents for the conveyance of property, as well as marriage contracts, leases and financial agreements. The legal profession had, by legislation at the beginning of the nineteenth century, finally creamed off the most lucrative side of their traditional business, their conveyancing monopoly, and the scriveners had become hired hacks attached to law stationers' offices. An expansion in Parliamentary Bills, and in share speculations during the railway boom of the 1830s, helped to keep the scribes busily at work, often day and night, at 8d a sheet.

By the 1860s some of the law stationers' offices were charging the unfortunate scrivener for his seat, where he sat in the outer office waiting for such work as came in during the day, and even withheld a proportion of his fees as a contribution towards the office running costs. Many took work home with them, anxious to earn as much as they could while the law courts were in session, to see them through the three long months of vacation each year. It became traditional for the scribes, out of work during the summer, to leave the city and help with hop-picking in the Kent countryside to make ends meet.

The scribe's job was perhaps more congenial than it seems at first sight, however. They certainly enjoyed an unfortunate reputation at this time as drunkards; and in a booklet on the law writer's trade, *Scribes Ancient and Modern* (1889), one W. Warrell hastened to excuse their reputation on the grounds that "constant anxiety occasioned by hurrying off work and working so much at night has a debilitating and disastrous effect on the nerves and the eyesight of the scribe. And it is to these causes coupled with the sedentary nature of their occupation, that their failing regarding drink is undoubtedly to be traced."

The "bruised and battered ruby-nosed Law Writers", whether they knew it or not, were the last surviving workman scribes in a long line of penpushers stretching all the way back to ancient Egypt. A list of tools provided in Warrell's booklet tallies remarkably closely with those used by medieval scribes, and the description of their use, too, echoes the preoccupations of the professional and monastic scribes in the long centuries before the advent of print. First on the list were quill pens— turkey feathers by this time, since they were stronger than goose and no doubt answered better to the demands of the industrial age—followed by a penknife. Curiously, the writer omits to mention its use for shaping the pen, and goes straight on to say that it was to be used for cutting out on parchment, and scratching out on paper (those ever-present mistakes). The knife should also have a smooth, bone handle to burnish down the writing surface which had been roughened by scratching out.

A pumice stone, for rubbing down the rough skin, is followed by a pounce rubber for taking up some of the greasiness from the surface of the parchment, and gum sandarac to inhibit the spread of ink. A pencil is mentioned, but again the first on the list of its uses is "to tick mistakes in engrossments and fair copies, discovered either on examination or when copying". The only other use mentioned is to mark the number of

Opposite. Initial letters
from Henry Shaw's *The
Handbook of Medieval
Alphabets and Devices*
(1853).

folios, presumably to keep count of the scribes' earnings. Ruler, apron
and pencase were followed by a departure from scribal tradition—a box
of "Three Holes" and a box of "Horse Shoes", types of steel pen nibs
which by this time had penetrated even the conservative Law Writers'
toolboxes.

An interesting gadget, supplied we are told by the employer, was a
"runner", a revolving wheel with sharp spikes equally spaced around its
circumference like a spur. This could be run down the side of a sheet of
parchment, against a ruler, and it would automatically prick out the
small marks required for accurately spaced lines. Following traditional
practice the parchment was folded, and the wheel pressed down through
two thicknesses at once, to make sure that the prick marks on each
facing sheet matched each other perfectly. This wheel method of prick-
ing may well have been used by medieval scribes, since it is such a simple
and useful idea, but no trace of the instrument or definite proof of its use
has yet come to light.

"Men," writes Warrell, "do not monopolise the whole business of
scribing; women have been introduced by one or two law stationers. No
objection ought to be made by any man to this innovation provided that
the women are paid at the same rate as the men." He does not disclose,
however, what women of the time thought about working in the
company of the free-drinking quill-drivers.

In the kind of conditions under which these hack scriveners often
worked, there were bound to be occasional lapses from duty. Their
excuses and the sorts of punishment they received were presumably
numerous enough to warrant the stereotyped labels which Warrell gives
them. To "Chuck", for example, covered a multitude of sins, of which
the most common was to take work home and bring it back uncom-
pleted. A "Royal Chuck" was the extreme of this misdemeanour, and
was committed when a scrivener took work home and brought it back
the following morning without even having unrolled it! To "Grass" was
the punishment meted out for failing to execute work properly: the de-
faulter was obliged to sit for a prescribed period ("put out to grass")
without work. The list of excuses for "Chucks" throws a pathetic light on
the domestic arrangements of some of the nineteenth-century Law
Writers: for example, "Been very sick all night. The brokers were put in
for debt. So cold I couldn't hold the pen." But: "I could not go on as I had
left my knife at the office" has a solid ring of practical truth about it.
Warrell tells us that "some scribes are like fishes out of water if they have
not their knife [in their left hand] for the purpose of holding down the
paper whilst writing". The medieval scribes, who were never depicted
without quill and knife in their hands, would have understood this excuse
very well, as should any modern practitioner of the craft.

Although styles of everyday handwriting changed very little in the
course of the nineteenth century, the art of the book on the other hand
was thoroughly revolutionised—by the developments in colour printing.
Multi-colour polychrome printing from woodblocks had become
greatly refined during the early part of the century, but the crucial
invention was made by Alois Senefelder (1771–1834), who in the 1790s

had been unable to afford to engrave the plates for an edition of some plays he had written, and stumbled upon the technique of lithographic printing using smooth absorbent stones. This involved taking a print from a drawing or painting made directly on to the surface of the stone, using a special greasy ink. No intermediate stages were required. Thus many of the restrictions placed on the artist by the engraving tool as used in copper and wood were removed. This direct process could be used to print thousands of prints using three, four or more colours. Monochrome prints could be hand-coloured, and indeed they were; but this was laborious and expensive. For the first time lithographic printing allowed large numbers of people to own books and prints in many colours.

This advance coincided with the Gothic revival which was enjoying immense popularity in Europe and America, with its idealised and romanticised concepts of medievalism which distance in time had made cosy and respectable. It was not just that medieval illuminated books were the only traditional models. Their opulence, and their largely religious content, must have made them seem the perfect subject for reproduction by chromolithography, and the carefully inscribed literary sentiments so beloved of the age completed the appropriateness of this vision—so successfully that, in the space of sixty years, framed texts and illuminated gift books appeared in many languages in houses and cottages all over the world. For all the fulminations of John Ruskin and William Morris about the glory and dignity of hand craftsmanship, the impact of those popular colour prints of "illuminations" was so great that, even after ninety years of "arts and crafts revival" in the graphic and other arts, from Melbourne to Kansas City or Berlin, calligraphy and illumination are still equated in most people's minds with those early colour-printed books and texts first made popular over one hundred and thirty years ago. Indeed, whatever the art historian and calligraphers of our own time may say to disparage the graphic products of the Victorian era, their immense continuing influence is undeniable.

The Victorian passion for the richness of the "illuminated book" printed by chromolithography and similar processes provided a ready market for the work of artists who made designs for the decorated pages of gift volumes. Many artists, from the 1820s to the end of the century, were attracted to the medium. Three British artists in particular, Henry Shaw, Owen Jones and Noel Humphreys, produced books on lettering and ornament which were greatly admired at the time and widely copied by amateurs. Shaw (1800–73) was an antiquarian and draughtsman whose style was essentially based on exhaustive and detailed copies of medieval originals. Ninety-five pages of his hand-painted facsimiles, for the most part on vellum, are preserved in the Victoria and Albert Museum in London, and he published a lettering source-book, *Alphabets, Numerals and Devices of the Middle Ages* (1845). Owen Jones (1809–74), an architect whose own press had done a great deal to set new standards in the art of colour printing, published two books in 1864 which were clearly aimed at the market provided by the enthusiastic amateur copyists: *One Thousand and One Initial Letters* and *Seven*

Hundred and Two Monograms were both published for the price of five shillings. Noel Humphreys (1810–79) also made exquisite illuminated books. In one of them, *The Parables of Our Lord*, completed in 1846, he gives us some insight into the mind and motives of a nineteenth-century illuminator.

> It has been the aim of the designer to render the ornamental border-ings of each page appropriate to the text, and to avoid all mere arbitrary or idle ornaments; and he has thought it more suitable that the garments of gold and many colours in which he has arranged them, should at all events be *new rather than embroidery borrowed from old missals or other sources of conventional orna-ment, however quaint and beautiful; and therefore, however far the illuminator may have fallen short of his intention, the designs will be found to be strictly original, fresh, and full of the purpose alone to which they are devoted.*

Nineteenth-century artists generally responded enthusiastically to the opportunities offered by the new colour-printing processes. Despite the fashionable emphasis on medievalism, their lettering styles were un-avoidably conditioned by generations of engraved copybooks; but as they drew on the stone with pointed pens or fine brushes they were freed by their place in time and the circumstances of a new medium to indulge in flights of fancy and exuberant and sentimental invention, with an impressive energy and commitment. But because their work was so far removed from the classical discipline of the broad-edged quill pen which had been the tool of Charlemagne's scribes, their printed letters did not possess the substance or spontaneity so essential for fine calligraphy. Medieval scripts made with a broad-edged pen were often carefully imitated and laboriously reconstructed, by outlining with a pointed pen and filling in by brush; this technique missed the essence even of the angular Gothic scripts—and in so doing it unfortunately misled generations of students who faithfully copied these copies.

Colour printing by the lithographic process did for lettering and illumination what the engraved copybooks of the sixteenth and later centuries did for calligraphy and handwriting. By "calling in the aid of the printer and lithographer for the rapid multiplication and dissemi-nation of beautiful specimens", Shaw, Owen Jones, Humphreys and the others—however high their standards of draftsmanship, printing or ideals, led their readers once again to imitate a machine-printed imita-tion of hand-work. Certainly Humphreys was a deeply committed and thoughtful artist, and in his manual *The Art of Illumination and Missal Painting* (1849) he described some of the qualities he felt an illuminator should cultivate. He should "have a feeling for poetry and the exquisite dreamings of fairy-land and delight in researches into the history of costumes, weapons and armour of all ages". After being well-prepared by these researches, "and with the air of assiduous application, the illuminator may lift his art to the high position which legitimately be-longs to it; but which the poor productions of the last century and a half had tended so greatly to lower; reducing that which should be an

The Art of Illumination and Missal Painting by Noel Humphreys was printed in full colour but with some parts left blank, so that the enthusiastic owner could hand-paint in the details himself.

Whatsoever thy hand findeth to do, do it with thy might;

Amateur penmanship, dating from about 1890. The letters were not written directly with a pen, but outlined and filled in with watercolour.

exquisite art, to a routine of the most vulgar mechanism." These words seem to carry an unfortunate echo of the rueful and defensive expressions of the early writing masters. Humphreys felt obliged to protest the legitimacy of his chosen art, and hinted at the weakness which really lies at the root of all the Victorian printed "illuminated" books. They were, after all, printed.

But who bought all the "How-to" manuals on illuminating and ornamental lettering or subscribed to periodicals like *The Illuminator's Magazine* (1861–62), or consulted gilding recipes for "those who have not the bladder of a sturgeon"? Digby Wyatt, author of *Illuminating, What it was, What it should be, How to Practise it* (1861), gives us some indication of the sort of people he had in mind as readers of his book. There was a wide field, he thought, for useful and even productive labour designing exquisite originals for reproduction by chromolithography and chromotypy; the blazoning of addresses, pedigrees and family records (another Victorian passion), and memorials; and illustrations for presentation or the transcripts of private authors. He even specifically suggested that "a mother could scarcely do a thing more likely to benefit her children and fix the lessons of love and piety which she would desire to plant in their memories, than to illuminate for them little volumes, which from their beauty or value they might be inclined to treasure for life". Even young people themselves, he went on, might benefit from transcribing worthy texts in this manner so as to encourage them to identify with "the best and highest class of sentiments".

This worthy (and wordy) little book also includes suggested verses which might be appropriately inscribed and hung in smoking rooms, still rooms, music rooms, store rooms, billiard rooms, justice rooms, casinos and even surgical museums!

We take no note of time
But for its loss;
To give it then a tongue
Is wise in man.

This little verse, suggested for the wall of a bell tower, gives us some idea of the awesome depths of sentiment and strangled poesy to which calligraphy and illumination were expected to plunge.

There must, of course, have been an enormous interest stimulated by the large numbers of illuminated and decorative books produced throughout the century. The British Museum supplied specially designed portable glass-topped cases for the use of students and amateurs, who loved to take out some of the most precious manuscripts in its collections, and sit in the manuscript room politely painting copies of them with their water-colours. The arrival of chromolithographically printed books coincided with an impressive growth of prosperity, and of a middle-class section of society with the leisure and income to indulge a recreational interest in the crafts, just as thousands of people today seek satisfaction and enjoyment out of creating things for themselves. It is interesting that as soon as people have leisure they immediately reveal a yearning to make things, to invent with their hands and eyes. The nineteenth-century middle classes turned for instruction to the manuals —and Digby Wyatt was once again ready for them with advice to designers of illumination:

> ... *eschew quaintness, and aim at beauty; let him not shrink from beauty in old times because it was marked in quaintness: but with a a discriminating eye let him learn to winnow the chaff from the wheat, and scattering the one to the winds, let him garner up the other in the storehouse of his memory, and for the sustenance of his artistic life.*

But there were others genuinely trying to come to terms with what seemed to them to be a legitimate art, but which had somehow lost its footing in a machine age; and the greatest of these was William Morris.

10. Writing as Art

By the middle of the century Great Britain, with the advantage of the start gained in the early Industrial Revolution, had become the most affluent nation in the world, leading the other Western nations along the apparently triumphant path of economic progress and growth. This was the age when the principles of capitalism were most triumphantly vindicated; and to represent this victory a series of immense rituals of self-congratulation took place: the great international exhibitions, at the "Crystal Palace" in London (1851), in Vienna (1854), in Paris (1855) and elsewhere. The largest and most ostentatious of all was the Philadelphia Centennial in 1876.

The "Great Exhibition of Works of Industry of All Nations" in 1851, planned and organised under Prince Albert's control, was designed to display the variety and ingenuity of British manufactures within the great Crystal Palace built for the purpose by Joseph Paxton in Hyde Park and such was their self-confidence that many other countries were invited to share the glittering stage. It was a huge success—fourteen thousand firms exhibited their products—and among its effects was a decision by the Prince Consort, with government support and financial backing, to purchase objects from it to form the foundation collection of a new Museum of Manufactures, which in 1852 first opened its doors to the public at Marlborough House. The museum was intended to encourage the study of sound principles of design in industry, and to represent the greatest achievements of mechanical and industrial manufacture.

But ironically, almost from the start, this new museum in praise of industrialism became infected with a strongly reactionary distaste for mechanisation, and its first director, Henry Cole, and his colleagues began to see their role more as the preservers of the older and more "real" design and manufacturing achievements of the pre-industrial age. By the time the Museum of Manufactures had been transformed into the Victoria and Albert Museum, in 1899, it had already become the world's foremost collection of such hand-made works of art and craft.

This curious reversal was echoed in the many newly founded Schools of Applied Art and Design throughout the country. A movement began, fed by John Ruskin's passionate idealism, which rejected the effects as well as the products of industrialisation, the human misery that accompanied it, and the alienation of working people from the objects of their labour. The leading prophet of this movement, William Morris (1834–96), like Ruskin before him was angered by the slavery of the spirit to which, it seemed to him, the machine subjected craftsmen and women in the factories; and in 1860, while still in his twenties, he founded an association of "fine-art" workmen and craftsmen whose aim

COPY No. I.   *After* WINCHESTER FORMAL WRITING about 975 A.D.

Et haec scribimus vobis ut gaudeatis, & gaudium vestrum sit plenum.

Et haec est annunciatio, quam audivimus ab eo, & annunciamus vobis: Quoniam Deus lux est, & tenebrae in eo non sunt ullae.

Winchester MS. v. slightly modified.

Heavy Italics based on Winchester MS.

Note: *This copy is written with a pen, not printed* Ef. 26. August 1919 A.D.

In order that a child may learn how to write well the teaching of handwriting should begin with the practice of a Formal Hand. This Manuscript is written with a BROAD-NIBBED PEN which makes the strokes thick or thin according to the direction in which it moves. The strokes are generally begun downwards or forwards & the letters are formed of several strokes (*the pen being lifted after each stroke*): thus *c* consists of *two* strokes, the first a long curve down, the second a short curve forward. The triangular 'heads' (as for *b* or *d*) are made by *three* strokes; 1st. a short thick curve down, 2nd. a short thin stroke up (*the nib for this stroke being placed on the beginning of the first and slid up to the right*), 3rd. the thick straight *stem* stroke of the letter itself down (*the pen for this stroke not being lifted*).

Broad-nibbed steel pens and Reeds may be used: Quill pens are very good but require special cutting. How to cut Quill and Reed pens may be learned from my Handbook "Writing & Illuminating, & Lettering" (*John Hogg, London*: 6s. 6d. *net*) besides how to make MS. Books and to write in colour.   Edward Johnston: *Ditchling, Sussex.*

THIS SHEET IS PUBLISHED BY DOUGLAS PEPLER at HAMPSHIRE HOUSE HAMMERSMITH 1916 A.D.

Price *Five Shillings*

Edward Johnston revived the simplicity of the Carolingian style, and used a 10th-century English hand as inspiration for much of his formal penmanship. This sample sheet was partly hand-printed and partly hand-written

was to make things simply, honestly and well by hand. He advocated a return to the standards of hand craftsmanship of an idealised medieval and rural life, and a slightly sentimental socialist philosophy.

What might have been a futile and unnoticed gesture against the inevitable processes of industrialisation and mechanisation was turned, by Morris's energy and powers of persuasion, into an arts-and-crafts revival which was to have a long-term and international influence (particularly in Germany and the U.S.A.), and whose reverberations are with us still. The appeal of this movement and its aesthetic principles, however, was never a mass one; that, alas, was a dream unrealised. But the affluent middle-class citizens of the newly-rich industrial countries were greatly attracted to the fresh quality of the hand-made artifacts which William Morris and his followers began to produce.

Among the many crafts in which Morris interested himself was the art of the book. Fine calligraphy, which earlier than most crafts had been defeated by its machine-made equivalent, the printing-press, was regarded by Morris as a legitimate branch of the fine arts, and by his influence the calligrapher gradually recovered for himself a more respected role—as an artist who "paints" with the shapes of letters, and makes them with a quill as well as a brush. Morris had no respect for the machine-made Gothic of the ornamental penmen, or for printed letters in imitation of calligraphy. If it was to be valid at all, calligraphy must speak for its own times and in its own right, just as did the chairs and silver, tapestries, stained glass and textiles which he made in his workshop in Red Lion Square. Noel Humphreys' work did to some extent satisfy these criteria; but it spoke for its own times, the mid-nineteenth century, and not for the new century which was about to begin.

Edward Johnston (1872–1944) studied medicine unhappily as a young man, and in his spare time dabbled with copying manuscripts in the British Museum, and inventing a few strains of his own. When he was invited to teach an evening class in illumination at the Central School of Arts and Crafts he was conscious that he knew only one important thing about calligraphy—which was that he knew nothing. But together with his students he began to learn, and by their earnest and minute researches into early techniques they began to revive skills in illuminating which had been lost for centuries. They experimented with methods of gilding, the preparation of vellum and parchment for writing, and the mixing of pigments for paints and inks. They brought back the use of the square-cut pen, and raised the standard of direct calligraphy from the depths to which succeeding mechanical processes had reduced it. Johnston's book *Writing and Illuminating, and Lettering*, written with the help and collaboration of his students and friends, spread and shared this knowledge across the world. It was first published in 1906, and is still in print today. Priscilla Johnston in her account of her father's life reminds us that he sought for the improvement of lettering and that calligraphy should have "a place among real things—in the simplest and best sense—as works of art".

It was one of Johnston's particular achievements to show that a master of traditional letter forms need not be other-worldly or backward-looking in spirit, and could create modern letters both as art and for everyday use. Between 1910 and 1930 he designed a series of letter types and initials which cut through centuries of muddle and affectation, including typefaces for Count Harry Kessler of the Cranach Press. When he designed a new typeface, a block-letter alphabet which has remained a classic example of simple clarity, for the London Transport system in 1916, he combined the elegant proportions of Roman carved letters with the no-nonsense detail of the Greek lapidary inscriptions which had no serifs or "feet". Many other "sans serif" letters have followed it, and today we are surrounded by such letters wherever we

FIG. 80.

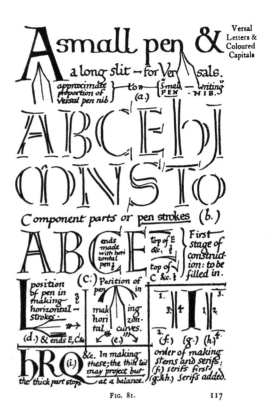

FIG. 81.

look, from motorway signs to magazines.

Interest in the graphic arts, and particularly in lettering and calligraphy, was developing rapidly in Europe too at this time. Rudolph von Larisch in Vienna and later Rudolph Koch in Offenbach were notably successful in improving standards. The traditional alphabets in Germany and Austria, as we have seen, had proceeded along different lines from the rest of Europe, retaining the use of the Gothic script right through the 1930s, and this gave a particular flavour to their approach. Von Larisch (1856–1934) was an official in the chancery of the Austrian Empire under Franz Joseph, and was thus able to study old manuscripts at first hand; and he was fired with an enthusiasm to improve the standards of handwriting which compared so badly with those of the past. He published a pamphlet entitled *Zierschriften im Dienst der Kunst* (Decorative writing in the service of art), and began to teach writing at the Vienna School of Art in 1902. In 1906, the year in which Edward Johnston's great work appeared, he published his most important book *Unterricht in Ornamentaler Schrift*, a manual of instruction in decorative writing and lettering. He was fascinated by the application of lettering to many different materials, such as glass, metal, wood and textiles; and believed that the pattern of written letters should seek to express some kind of harmony and an expression of emotional unity.

Johnston emphasised the direct and spontaneous use of the broad-edged pen, rather than meticulous imitation with a fine point; and he returned to medieval methods as well as models.

WIE IM HIMMEL ALSO AUCH
AUF ERDEN · UNSER TÄGLICH
BROT GIB UNS HEUTE · UND VER-
GIB UNS UNSRE SCHULD / WIE
WIR VERGEBEN UNSERN SCHUL-
DIGERN · UND FUEHRE UNS
NICHT IN VERSUCHUNG SON

Rudolph Koch, like Johnston, took his inspiration from traditional methods; but both the tapestry (*opposite*) and the detail from the opening of a manuscript book (*above*) show that he could produce work that is emphatically of its own time.

The link between German and English calligraphy was strengthened when Anna Simons (1871–1951), who came from a Prussian legal family, came to London and studied in Johnston's class in 1901, becoming one of his best students. After returning home she published a German translation of *Writing and Illuminating, and Lettering* (1910), and later of his second portfolio, *Manuscript and Inscriptional Letters*. She also helped with an exhibition of calligraphy in Germany arranged by the Calligraphers' Society, which had been founded by Johnston and his fellow scribes around 1910. Enthusiasm for lettering and typographic design in German-speaking countries was thus greatly helped by the craft movement which had stemmed from William Morris's revival.

There were of course the usual schisms, including a famous long-standing dispute between Johnston and one of his students, Graily Hewitt, who had contributed information on gilding to his book; although this was finally settled. Eric Gill, another of Johnston's students, was one of the founders of a craft fraternity which ended in acrimonious dispute over financial affairs.* Even the Calligraphers' Society, of which Johnston was president, foundered after a few years of what he himself described as "its stormy history". But the Society of Scribes and Illuminators, founded by Johnston's students in 1922, still flourishes today, with the aim of encouraging high standards in the art of calligraphy.

Rudolph Koch of Offenbach (1874–1934) was a skilled calligrapher with close ties with type and type-design. He worked at the Klingspor type foundry and taught lettering at the School of Arts and Crafts in Offenbach. Under his leadership a group was formed in 1918 called the Offenbach Penmen, which later became a workshop community where Koch and his assistants worked in such crafts as lettering, woodcuts, embroidery, weaving, block-books printed on Japanese paper, and

---

*The disagreements did however produce a bonus for some of the more discerning of the Guild's neighbours. They rescued for posterity hand-printed broadsheets and illustrated book pages which had been meant for the flames of a bonfire of proofs and prints cleared out from the Guild's St Dominic's Press, when Douglas Pepler the printer finally broke away to set up the Ditchling Press.

ICH BIN DER HERR DEIN GOTT · DU SOLLST KEI
NE ANDERN GOETTER NEBEN MIR HABEN · DU
SOLLST DIR KEIN BILDNIS NOCH IRGENDEIN GLEICH
NIS MACHEN WEDER DES DAS OBEN IM HIM
MEL NOCH DESS DAS UNTEN AUF ERDEN ODER
DESS DAS IM WASSER IST BETET SIE NICHT
AN UND DIENET IHNEN NICHT · DENN ICH DER
HERR DEIN GOTT BIN EIN EIFRIGER GOTT DER
DA HEIMSUCHET DER VAETER MISSETAT AN
DEN KINDERN BIS AN DAS DRITTE UND VIERTE
GLIED · DU SOLLST DEN NAMEN DES HERRN DEI
NES GOTTES NICHT MISSBRAUCHEN DENN DER HERR
WIRD DEN NICHT UNGESTRAFT LASSEN DER SEINEN
NAMEN MISSBRAUCHT · DU SOLLST DEN FEIERTAG HEI
LIGEN · SECHS TAGE SOLLST DU ARBEITEN UND ALLE DEIN
DINGE BESCHICKEN ABER AM SIEBENTEN IST DER TAG
DES HERRN DEINES GOTTES · DU SOLLST DEINEN VATER
UND DEINE MUTTER EHREN AUF DASS DU LANGE
LEBEST IM LANDE DAS DIR DER HERR DEIN GOTT
GIBT · DU SOLLST NICHT TOETEN · DU SOLLST
NICHT EHEBRECHEN · DU SOLLST NICHT STEHLEN
DU SOLLST KEIN FALSCH ZEUGNIS REDEN WIDER DEI
NEN NAECHSTEN · LASS DICH NICHT GELUESTEN DEI
NES NAECHSTEN HAUS · LASS DICH NICHT GELUESTEN
DEINES NAECHSTEN WEIB KNECHT MAGD VIEH NOCH ALLES
WAS SEIN IST ✠

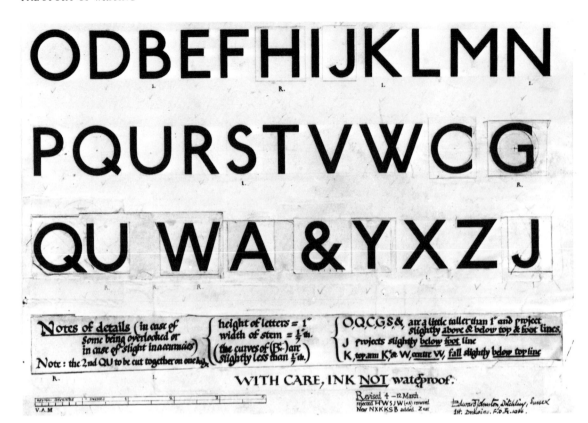

ODBEFHIJKLMN
PQURSTVWCG
QU WA &YXZJ

Johnston created a simple alphabet in 1916 which is still in use today by London Transport.

metalwork; and all of them were trained in lettering. Many of them went on to become leading teachers and practitioners in Germany, Austria, America and England; and their influence has made a great contribution to the improvement of letter shapes and type design throughout the world.

A calligrapher trained in these new schools could thus be designer, craftsman, typographer and graphic artist—several professions in one—catering for the everyday needs of the fast moving world of modern communications; and at the same time a fine artist using letters as a medium for personal and private expression. As always, only a small proportion of such work reaches the height of artistry and excellence—and art was often a by-product anyway, good workmanship inspired with a spark of individuality and life. William Morris's contemporaries certainly thought of themselves merely as honest workmen, for whom art should be a by-product of function and utility.

The ideal of "beauty through usefulness", however, may have been overplayed in the arts and crafts movement. Edward Johnston may have worked on designs for labels for a patent laxative medicine, but he is not remembered for that. Although calligraphy provides a fine basis for a graphic design training, the work of Edward Johnston and his European counterparts made it possible for it to become an art form in its own right: the search for the marriage of words to form as an expression of the self, a performance.

160

Whosoever thou art that enterest this Church leave

The prejudice which inhibits us from seeing Western calligraphy as art is transcended by the strength and lively spirit in this detail from Johnston's writing. Black and red, bamboo and steel pen on paper, 1938.

In nineteenth-century Japan, as today, calligraphy was regarded as a fine art rather than a handicraft. The printing press no doubt had had less impact on such an unwieldy written language; but it was traditionally accepted that only a privileged few would ever acquire the skill to write beautifully, and that even fewer would achieve artistic mastery. Where calligraphy was the pastime of princes and the spiritual expression of an exalted and revered priesthood, the kind of reforming zeal which William Morris and his friends had to bring to the rescue of calligraphy in the West was never needed.

The impressionist painter Vincent Van Gogh used everyday objects—bowls of flowers, chairs, tables, carpets—as the subject of his paintings, and moved them around within a rectangle on a flat canvas surface, choosing size and weight and rearranging the space between them and their colour relationships. He pursued a harmony, or indeed disharmony, imposing his own wishes upon the objects of his own choice, painting and repainting with brush and oil paint on the canvas.

A calligrapher, too, takes everyday objects—letters—and assembles them within a rectangular surface. He pushes and pulls them around, choosing different weights and sizes, placing them in different relationships with each other, colouring them and manipulating them in space. There is the same search for harmony or disharmony of his own choosing. Letters and words, like Van Gogh's chairs, are merely the starting point for an exploration in space. Of course their literary function, the shapes of words and the beautiful forms of letters which have slowly evolved over human history, will influence his choices. But he is free to invest these marks with as much life as his skill allows and with as much sensitivity as his soul possesses. He paints with words.

11. Personality and the Pen

The portable pen for modern needs – but the early pens were by no means as reliable as some of their advertisements claimed.

In the winter of 1806 the poet William Wordsworth wrote to his hosts, Sir George and Lady Beaumont, what he called "the longest letter I ever wrote in my life" (it was 18 pages long). "I shall not," he said, "be able to keep it up to the end in this style, notwithstanding I have the advantage of writing with one of your *steel pens,* with which Miss Wordsworth has just furnished me." He did not say that it was his enthusiasm for writing with such a convenient instrument which inspired him, but we may be sure that the effect of the new pen must have been a contributory factor, as anyone acquiring a new pen today can confirm.

Yet the first recorded mention of a fountain pen, as we have seen, is far from recent. According to Albertine Gaur, in her booklet *Writing Materials of the East,* the Caliph al-Mu'izz in the tenth century AD asked for a pen "capable of carrying its own supply of ink, where the ink would flow only when the pen was used for writing. So at other times it could safely be carried in his sleeve without fear of soiling his clothes". His craftsmen finally presented him with the fountain pen he desired, made in pure gold.

But it was not until the nineteenth century, when the need arose for an improvement on the quill for general use, that progress was made in designing a portable writing instrument "with a reservoir . . . to supply ink for some time without replenishing" (as the *Penny Cyclopaedia* of 1840 put it).

It was not enough simply to fill a tube at one end with ink, put a cork in it, and let it leak out at the other. Certainly the essence of a fountain pen is the principle of the "controlled leak"; but just how to control that leak was the technical question to which many ingenious inventors applied their minds.

The issues involved were succinctly put by James P. Maginnis in a lecture to the Royal Society of Arts in 1905:

> When a filled pen is held point downward, the ink it contains is acted on by a variety of forces, among which may be reckoned gravity, inertia, capillary attraction, air pressure, friction, and the viscosity of the liquid as well as several minor forces. If the pen is properly made, these forces are in a state of equilibrium, and the ink does not run out of the reservoir. As soon, however, as the point touches the surface it is capable of wetting, the action of the capillary attraction is altered, with the result that the ink is enabled to flow from the reservoir, and that the pen writes. A fountain pen, to be perfect, should fulfil certain requirements. It should be of convenient form and size and as light as possible. Its ink carrying capacity should be as large as is consistent with its portability. It

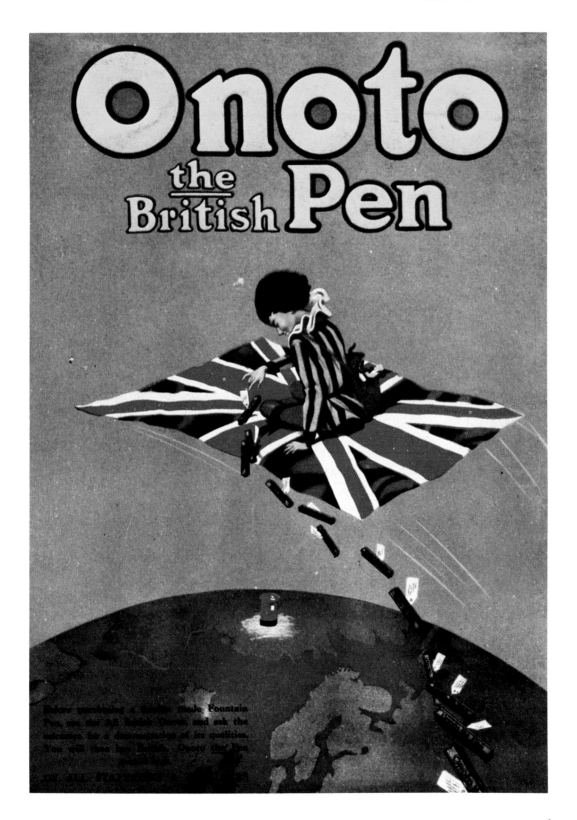

Write to them with a Parker

A fountain pen is indispensable at holiday time—and the Parker Duofold is the best of all pens. It is always ready to write—any-time—anywhere. It carries more ink than most pens. It never hesitates or splutters or scratches, for the velvet smooth Parker Duofold point is guaranteed to give 25 years' faithful service, while the barrel and cap of Parker 'Permanite' is practically un-breakable. If you haven't got a Parker Duofold, go to the nearest pen shop before you go on your holiday, and try a few Parker Pens. Any good dealer will be pleased to let you test as many as you like without any obligation.

4 COLOURS 4 SIZES

Black-tipped lacquer red, jade green, or lapis lazuli blue, or plain black.

Senior	...	30/-
Special	...	25/-
Junior	...	21/-
Lady	...	21/-

Pencils to match pens
17/6   15/-   12/6

Parker Pens are Empire Made.

THE PARKER PEN COMPANY LTD., BUSH HOUSE, STRAND, W.C.2.

The company founded by George Parker had be-come, by the end of the 1930s, the leader of the fountain pen industry.

should not be ready to empty itself, except when required to do so, then only at a rate not exceeding the requirements of the writer. It should be prompt in delivering ink the instant the nib touches the paper. It should have as few working parts as possible ... free from complication or liability to injure it from careless handling.

It was not until the end of the nineteenth century that fountain pen manufacturers began to make large quantities by machine. There was some resistance at first to their products—as there had been to steel pens—and many were far from reliable. At least one man, George S. Parker, who later founded The Parker Pen Company, started in business after being forced to modify the unsatisfactory fountain pens supplied to his students at the School of Telegraphy in Janesville, Wisconsin, in the early days of this century. Other manufacturers had worked on the problem of securing an even ink-flow, but it was clear that there was still sufficient room for improvement to cause him to experiment for himself in the hotel bedroom where he was living as a poorly paid teacher. By the end of the 1930s he had become the leader of the American fountain pen industry.

For in those days, even before the mechanics of the pens had been perfected, manufacturers had tended to concentrate, as had their Victorian forefathers in the stick pen industry, on decoration. There was little variety or competition in the pen points themselves, but the manufacturers vied with each other in the production of decorative barrels in every conceivable form and style of finish. They were black and mottled brown, plain, chased, gold-banded and filigreed, cylindrical, hexagonal and octagonal; and some were even "barrelled", tapered like a cigar at both ends. But amidst this variety they almost all had one thing in common—they would not write reliably. An equally bewildering array of solutions to the problem of ensuring a steady ink flow were embodied in these pens, but most of them were in vain. They might write steadily for a while, but would soon either dry up or "flood".

One of the earliest manufacturers and inventors was Lewis Edson Waterman, who as an insurance salesman in the 1870s recognised the need for a writing instrument which helped speed up the process of getting people to sign on the "dotted line"; and from this practical consideration grew a very successful and practical fountain pen. In the last twenty years of the nineteenth century at least four European companies patented new fountain or "stylographic" pens; but America remained the chief battleground for the emergent warring manufacturers.

Most of the earliest fountain pens required their barrels to be filled with ink from a dropper. The part of the pen which held the nib was then screwed into the barrel, and the ink flowed out when the nib was flexed. These were the so-called "standard" pens. Other more carefully made versions were the "safety", specially designed to prevent leakage, and the "self-filler" which had a device for sucking up the ink into the barrel.

Then, as now, the public cared very little about the detailed mechanics of fountain pens, and judged them on more personal grounds. One pen will fit one temperament and handwriting style which another will not. The "feel" of a pen is very important to its user, and the early fountain pen makers went to great pains to recreate the flexibility to which users of both the quill and the steel nib were accustomed.

Even the Salvation Army endorsed and marketed a fountain pen of its own, called the "Post". It was by all accounts a sensible, efficient and ingenious writing instrument, but the Salvationists were less concerned with marketing pens than with other enterprises, and what might have been a well-deserved commercial success was never realised. The collapsible rubber tube and lever pens introduced later were another improvement, although the problems of flooding and drying-up were ever present. Yet by the 1920s Parker felt able to advertise a new pen in which these faults were now "impossible".

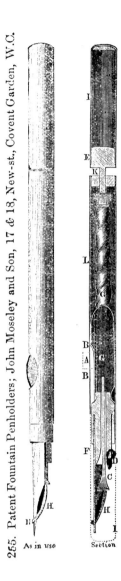

255. Patent Fountain Penholders; John Moseley and Son, 17 & 18, New-st., Covent Garden, W.C.

As in use   Section

Multi-coloured plastics developed by the Du Pont company revolutionised the appearance of fountain pens and pencils in the 1920s.

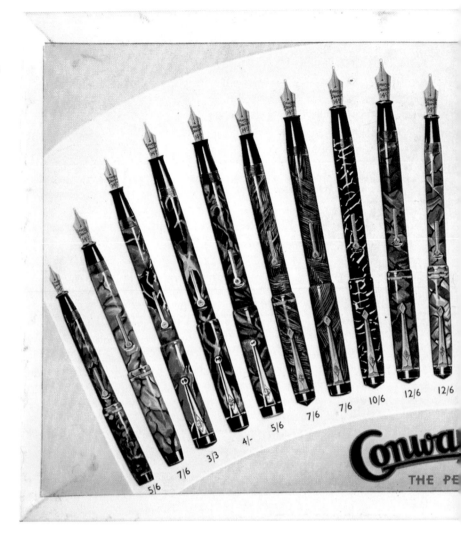

Until this time the base material for the barrels of most pens was hard rubber, shaped and threaded on hand-operated rubber-turning lathes. Even the name on the barrel was stamped on by a manually operated roller-type stamping machine. But in 1924 a new plastic marketed by the Du Pont company in tubular form in hundreds of different colours and combinations, began to revolutionise the appearance of fountain pens; in order, however, to focus public attention on a specific "family" of their own design the manufacturers were forced to reduce the bewildering array of patterns. Parker, for instance, reduced the number of models it produced from over 400 to less than thirty when they introduced their "Duofold" in 1922. By the mid-twenties most quality writing instruments were being made by the big four of the pen industry: Watermans, Parker, Shaeffer and Wahl (the "Eversharp"). In 1932 Parker introduced a "vacumatic" pen which for the first time boasted the now famous arrow-style pocket clip; and by the end of the decade the company had

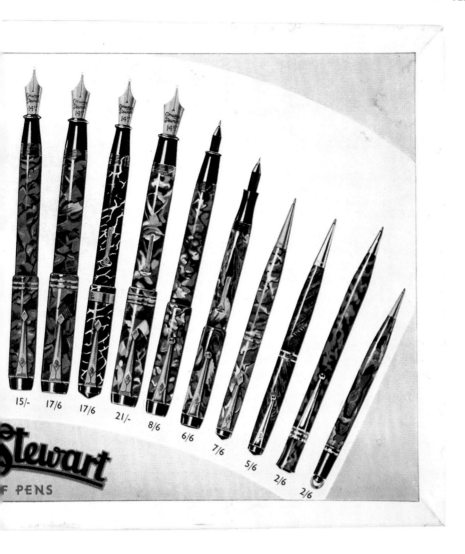

become the leading manufacturer in the world. Shaeffer's "white dot" (Lifetime) pens also provided a reliable service; and by the 1940s it could be said that there was little to choose among the pens on the market other than styling and appearance, a white dot or a blue diamond. But in January 1941 Parker introduced a major improvement, called simply the "51". The nib was partly covered by a special hood which enabled an ink to be used containing a quickly evaporating solvent which wrote "dry" with a wet ink. Shaeffer brought out a beautifully made pen of their own in the following year, and in 1943 Eversharp brought out a competitor too.

In 1945, however, a Chicago industrialist named Middleton Reynolds developed and was the first to market a new pen which in sheer volume of numbers quickly overtook the fountain pen: it was based on the ball-point principle. At much the same time the Hungarian refugee Laszlo Biro invented a ball-point pen in Argentina. As we have now begun to

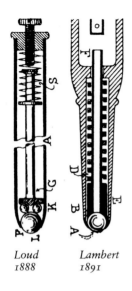

Loud
1888

Lambert
1891

expect, they were not the first to experiment with this principle, for as early as 1888 J. J. Loud had patented a pen designed as a marking instrument for boxes and rough surfaces. The ball revolved freely in the mouth of a tube which was held in position by two smaller balls and a spring-loaded plunger, which had to be screwed tight to prevent the ink leaking out. Another version of this idea was patented in 1891 by a Mr Lambert. The problem with the first ball-point pens was to find an ink of the right viscosity; and what Biro and Reynolds worked on is still the essential basis of ball-point ink—an oil-based ink which flows much more slowly than water-based ink.

In other respects the mechanism is very simple: on the inside of the tip, which retains the ball, there are six tiny channels, along which the ink is fed under pressure or gravity to the revolving spherical ball.

Two even more recent types of writing instrument have attracted widespread popularity—fibre-tip and floating-ball pens. Neither of them involves any major technical advance on the fountain pen, and indeed the latter is merely a fountain-pen with a revolving ball point, whose working parts are disposable. A multi-million dollar industry is built on persuading the public that the barrel or "housing" of the pen is more important than its "refill", its working parts, which often have to be thrown away when the ink in them has been used, but there are ways of circumventing this necessity, at least with cartridge-filled pens.

There are, in essence, four possible ways of slowing down and controlling the flow of ink, of dealing with the problem of the "controlled leak". The first is to control the consistency of the ink itself, whether thicker and more viscous, as is the case with ball-points, or more volatile like the spirit-based inks which dry on contact with the air, as with fibre-tip pens. Secondly, the aperture through which the ink escapes can be made smaller, and the accuracy of modern machining techniques has made much finer apertures possible with all kinds of pen. Thirdly, in the barrel where the ink is stored devices can be inserted to increase the surfaces over which the ink has to pass on its way to the tip, and thereby control the rate of capillary attraction. This method is employed in modern fountain and floating-ball pens. Finally, the capillary action can be slowed by storing the ink in an absorbent spongy material, as in the case of fibre-tip pens.

The fibre-tip pen, of course, differs very little in principle from the reed brush used five thousand years ago by the Egyptian scribes; and the fountain pen works in much the same way as a quill or reed. The ball-point gives us the kind of linear mark that the stylus made on the ubiquitous wax tablet of classical and medieval times; and the floating ball with its free-flowing water-based ink produces a mark that falls somewhere between the ball-point and the fountain pen. Thus the personal writing instruments we can buy today, whether expensive and valuable or throw-away and disposable, are still based on the simple principles of the writing sticks of our ancestors.

After Edward Johnston's success in helping to create an increased awareness of the virtues of formal handwriting, it was natural that

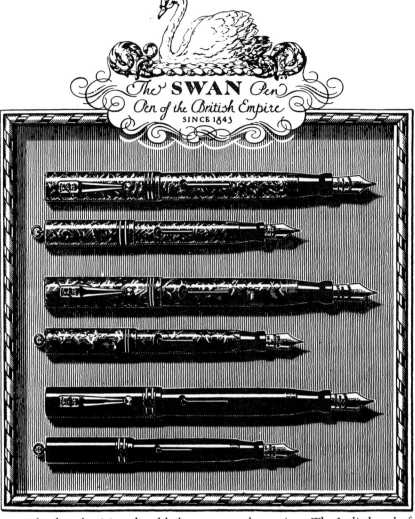

These pens already look dated, but the nib mechanism differs very little in principle from the ancient reed pen which the Greeks introduced.

everyday handwriting should also come under review. The Italic hand of the humanist scribes was singled out as a worthy model, in a sense thereby leap-frogging the intervening centuries which had been so dominated by the engraver's art. Alfred Fairbank set about with reforming zeal to make his own particular contribution to the revival of this style of writing for more general use. His early writing cards, the first of which was published in 1932, were the first of many Italic cursive exemplars which were to follow, and his handwriting manual published in the same year still continues to encourage the introduction of the Italic hand into a great number of schools in many countries throughout the world, as does the international Society for Italic Handwriting founded with his support in 1952.

Today, in the age of the ball-point, it may be less clear what model a child should follow, for the ball-point in its present shape is ill-suited to the shaded forms of the square-cut quill. Indeed it produces a mark much more closely related to the scratched letters on the walls of

Pompeii or on tablets of wax than to the classical scripts of Arrighi, Palatino and Cresci or for that matter the fruity flourishes of Messrs Cocker and Bickham. But we may yet have more leisure to consider the matter than we think . . .

> *In the present year many rumours are rife that a machine called a "Type-Writer", will supersede the scribe. I have seen it at work, and the operator, a lady, informs me that she can get through 40 folios per hour.*

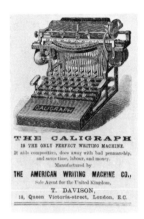

THE CALIGRAPH
IS THE ONLY PERFECT WRITING MACHINE.
It aids composition, does away with bad penmanship, and saves time, labour, and money.
Manufactured by
THE AMERICAN WRITING MACHINE CO.,
Sole Agent for the United Kingdom,
T. DAVISON,
18, Queen Victoria-street, London, E.C.

So wrote the anguished law writer Mr Warrell in 1889. What would he have said today, with telephones, typewriters, electronic word processors, computers, which at the touch of a key can produce 2,000 typed letters per hour? It may be that the increased efficiency of mechanical forms of communication will remove the urgent need to scribble as much as we all do nowadays. We no longer chat by letter so often as our parents did. But we all know that the "feel" of a writing instrument and the kind of mark it makes affect our attitude to the act of writing itself. Alfred Fairbank wrote that handwriting was "a system of movement involving touch"; and indeed the feel of the pen, the feel of the paper and the flow of the ink affect the way our thoughts and feelings flow. Many of us do not even like our own handwriting. It is like being forced to wear someone else's out-of-date clothes. It does not reflect the way we feel about ourselves, it is not us.

It is scarcely surprising that many of us have outgrown our own handwriting since we learned to form letters and join them up when we were children, and have done very little about our writing since except to make excuses for it. Yet, if we sat down as adults, with almost any one of the handwriting copybooks which can be easily acquired, and gave thought to how we form our letters and to the more natural joins which link them, we could reform our handwriting in an afternoon. We may not become calligraphers; but there are few crafts we could embark on which require so little expenditure on tools.

Even though we improve our handwriting, we will still be unable to conceal a great deal about our character and feelings every time we write. Tired or happy, young or old, our handwriting is as unique as our fingerprints. It cannot fail to speak for us and so for our time.

Indeed, once we accept that calligraphy, the art of beautiful writing, is a medium for self-expression it is hard to avoid the conclusion that our personal handwriting must reveal our character in a way which can be categorised and analysed by others. Since all individual gestures and expressive movements stem from our personality, writing can be no exception: an exposure of our character in graphic form.

The word graphology was coined in the mid-nineteenth century by the Abbé Jacques-Hippolyte Michon, whose pioneer studies in France sparked off a great deal of interest, particularly in Germany towards the end of the century, where Dr Ludvig Klages, a philosopher, published five books on the subject. Indeed it is still considered a valid subject for study in German universities today, where it is included in many medical and psychology courses. It is also a commonplace tool in the business of

AND I TURNED TO SEE THE VOICE THAT SPAKE TO ME

AND IN THE MIDST OF THE ... CANDLESTICKS ... SON OF MAN ... HIS COUNTENANCE WAS AS THE SUN ... as the sun shineth in his strength

I am Alpha and Omega the first and the last ... what you see write in a book

IN THE BEGINNING GOD CREATED THE HEAVEN AND THE EARTH AND THE EARTH WAS WITHOUT FORM AND VOID and darkness was upon the face of the deep And the Spirit of God moved upon the face of the waters And God said LET THERE BE LIGHT AND THERE WAS LIGHT And God saw the light that it was good and God divided the light from the darkness AND GOD CALLED THE LIGHT DAY AND THE DARKNESS HE CALLED NIGHT AND THE EVENING AND THE MORNING WERE THE FIRST DAY

personnel selection, where handwriting is used as part of the process of character assessment. Naturally, much is made of the signatures of famous people, for the sake of popularising the subject, but this often detracts from the serious consideration of this branch of research. Our handwriting can show a great deal, and quite startling examples of early diagnoses of both mental and physical disorders have been recorded by graphologists, proving that it can be a considerable help in preventive health care.

Writing can thus be a form of communication on many levels, from painting with words—calligraphy—to our own personal everyday script. But because familiarity is the basis of legibility, an agreement between writer and reader to attach the same significance to a similar mark, innovation for a calligrapher must be a matter of degree, of balance

This panel is written and illuminated by the author on calfskin vellum, with powdered gold, and gold leaf on gum and on burnished gesso. The pigments and carbon ink, written with a quill, differ little from the tools and materials used a thousand years ago.

Every time we write we reveal something of ourselves, and each mark is as individual as a section of our fingerprint.

between new and established forms. We do not invent completely new symbols, but like Van Gogh with his chairs we arrange and rearrange the old ones, shaping and reshaping them largely within the limits which 5,000 years of evolution have placed upon us.

The traditional tools of the scribe still have their place in the modern world. The calligrapher's craft depends on an intimate partnership between the three basic elements: the writing-instrument, the ink and the surface. A great deal of energy, beauty and life can be concentrated in mere thousandths of an inch at the tip of a pen. Calligraphy is meant to be viewed close to, as near as it was to the eye of the artist when he made it. Its enjoyment is an intimate experience, and the scale of the work is very fine. It depends a lot for its attraction on the vivid contrast between the superfine sharpness of a thin line and the gradual turn of the pen to a fat black. It is because I want the greatest possible measure of control over the mark which the pen makes that I make my own quills out of feathers, and use a free-flowing Chinese stick ink of finely ground carbon held together with gum, mixed freshly each time I write. And I still use vellum because of the fidelity its velvety nap imparts to the marks I make. It also has a special feel which, in conjunction with the sensitive pliability of the quill and the free-flowing ink, encourages the free flow of my visual intentions.

But even within these limitations we cannot avoid creating things which are of our own time. Italic, Gothic, Rustic and Carolingian are only small families which are part of a much larger tribe of Western letter forms. To us today their labels are less important than their shapes and their personalities. What inspired a previous generation may bore us. Each of us views traditional sources from a unique position within our generation, and we choose as our starting point whatever traditional form will best express our response to the text we are to write. History, therefore, presents us with an array of choices just like the colours in an artist's palette.

For a formal piece of writing, a royal document or something to mark

VISUAL SPACE IS UNIFORM,

visual space is uniform,

VISUAL SPACE IS UNIFORM CONTINUOUS AND CONTAINED·VISUAL
SPACE IS UNIFORM CONTINUOUS AND CONTAINED·VISUAL SPACE

continuous & contained

VISUAL SPACE IS UNIFORM, CONTINUOUS AND CONTAINED

a ceremonial occasion, we might choose a letter form with an "important" feel to it, something strong and upright perhaps, with definitely formed feet to each of the strokes. Every letter would stand aloof, without joins to its neighbours. It stands there with collar and tie and with polished black shoes. For a light-hearted poem we might decide to use the open-necked shirt and bare-foot informality of a cursive Italic script which dances hand in hand with its neighbours in a line. These choices influence the whole appearance of a page. The "colour" provided by the texture of formal lettering would be completely different because of the cumulative density of the details, and the stems, arches and serifs impart a darker and richer feel to the page. Informal writing will look paler, with less substance as it skips along.

Every time we make a black mark on the surface of a page we alter the shape of all the space which remains around it. It is just the same as taking one marble out of a jarful—the relationships between all of the rest are changed too. The permutations of texture are infinite. The use of gold and colour adds yet another dimension in contrast to the pattern of black written forms.

I believe there is artistry in everyone. A clean piece of paper in front of us still presents us with the chance to "turn over a new leaf", just as it did when we were schoolchildren presented with a new exercise book. We do not have to be professional opera singers to enjoy singing in the bath, and writing, after all, is everyman's craft. Pen, ink and paper provide us with an opportunity to rediscover some of the simple rewards which come from exploration, and, like the cave painters of Lascaux and Altamira 30,000 years ago, we don't have to leave our fireside to do it.

The families of letter-shapes, like so many colours in an artist's palette, await our choice – to be arranged and re-arranged to create mood and feeling.